How to Learn Anything Quickly

An Accelerated Program for Rapid Learning

Ricki Linksman

A Citadel Press Book
Published by Carol Publishing Group

A Citadel Press Book.
Published by Carol Publishing Group
Citadel Press is a registered trademark of Carol Communications, Inc.

Editorial, sales and distribution, rights and permissions inquiries
should be addressed to Carol Publishing Group, 120 Enterprise Avenue, Secaucus, N.J. 07094

In Canada: Canadian Manda Group, One Atlantic Avenue, Suite 105, Toronto, Ontario M6K 3E7

Carol Publishing Group books may be purchased in bulk at special discounts for sales promotion, fund-raising, or educational purposes. Special editions can be created to specifications. For details, contact Special Sales Department, 120 Enterprise Avenue, Secaucus, N.J. 07094.

Manufactured in the United States of America.
10 9 8 7 6 5 4 3 2 1

Library of Congress Cataloging-in-Publication Data

Linksman, Ricki, 1952–
    How to learn anything quickly : an accelerated program for rapid learning / Ricki Linksman.
        p.   cm.
    "A Citadel Press book."
    Includes bibliographical references and index.
    ISBN 0-8065-1792-1 (pbk.)
    1. Learning, Psychology of.   2. Accelerated learning.
3. Cognitive styles.   I. Title.
LB1060.L535   1996
370.15'23—dc20   96-46094
                                                         CIP

To humanity in the hope that all people make the fullest use of
    their God-given abilities,
to all my teachers who shared their knowledge so freely,
to my parents, Herb and Sheila Friedberg, who accelerated my
    own learning,
to my husband, Jay, for his love and encouragement,
and to God for allowing me to share His many gifts to me with
    the world.

Acknowledgments

This book is a product of a long, twenty-five year journey into the human mind and how people think and learn. I would like to acknowledge the many teachers I had along the way who took the leap into exploring unknown territory in the field of learning. Professors and instructors in the education field who have inspired me to find new ways of teaching include Dr. Robert Postman, Ph.D. of Hunter College of City University of New York, who taught me to explore new ways of reaching students; Dr. Emmy Lou Widmer, Ph.D. of Florida Atlantic University, who stressed "the match"—matching teaching techniques to the learner and recognizing that different techniques work for different people; Loretta Mione, reading instructor, Nova University, who taught me the components that make up an excellent reading program; and Barbara Meister Vitale, author of *Unicorns Are Real: A Right-Brained Approach to Learning* and a pioneer in brain research, who in 1980 personally trained me into the application of brain hemispheric preference and learning style research to the field of education. For fifteen years I have been developing new techniques to teach people of all ages in all subjects using learning styles and brain hemispheric preference and have verified time and again the success of the methods to accelerate learning. I would also like to thank Joe Hastenstab, Steve Barkley, and the staff of Performance Learning Systems for the training I received from them and their instructors in facilitation and presentation skills in training professionals to become more effective educators and trainers.

I would also like to thank my publisher, Steven Schragis of Carol Publishing Group, for his far-sighted vision in publishing this work; my editor, Marcy Swingle, for her assistance; and the wonderful staff at Carol Publishing including Renata Somogyi, Chris Thornton, and Helen Burr for their help with proofreading and production.

I would like to particularly acknowledge all my students, of all ages, with whom I had the privilege to work over the years, for they have taught me the numerous ways in which people learn.

I would like to thank my parents, Herb and Sheila Friedberg, who valued education and exposed me to a wealth of learning experiences that shaped my own life.

Special thanks to my husband, Jay Linksman, for his support, encouragement, and love.

Contents

Introduction: You CAN Learn Anything Quickly

Do you find it hard to keep up with change? Are constant innovations at your place of employment forcing you to spend time continually learning new skills or learning to use new technological equipment? Do you wish you could learn the skills required at your job more rapidly? Do you need to pass a training course or examination and wish you could reduce your study time? Do you feel your test scores do not reflect the great amount of time you spend studying? Do you find yourself frustrated by the slow speed at which you learn? Do you feel so hopeless that you don't think you can learn much at all?

Take heart! There is a way to learn anything you want, rapidly and successfully. Advances in science, particularly neuroscience, have helped us to better understand the way the brain works. Although this knowledge has been in laboratories, research centers, and scientific journals for years, few people have applied it to make our everyday lives easier. Some of these advances have gradually become public knowledge over the past decade. Unfortunately, our educational system is still in the dark ages when it comes to these advanced learning techniques. This book gives every person a method by which to learn successfully and quickly. It is written for everyone: for people of all ages, at all levels of education. It is designed to help every person learn quickly.

You will learn a technique that can be applied to learning any field you choose. Once you have mastered it, you will be able to use this method for the rest of your life for anything you wish to learn. This book will help you find the path to accelerated learning—a study method that works best for you.

So sit back and relax. Follow the simple steps in the book and you will emerge from the last page an expert on how *you* learn best and how to apply it to any field you want.

What Is a Superlink?

We each have a different way of learning. Each of us has a **superlink** that makes learning easier, faster, and more comfortable. Your superlink is the easiest method for you to take in information from the world in order to understand it, remember it, and retain it; it links information to our brain in a superfast way. Your superlink is a combination of your best learning style and the side of the brain you use to process and store information. Each of us learns differently. Some remember what they read, whereas others remember what they hear. Your learning style is the way *you* receive information from the world. There are four main learning styles: visual, auditory, tactile, and kinesthetic. **Visual learners** learn by seeing printed or graphic material or their surroundings. **Auditory learners** learn best by listening and talking. **Tactile learners** learn best by touching objects, experiencing the material emotionally, or by using their hands and fingers. **Kinesthetic learners** learn best by moving their large motor muscles. There are also people who use two, three, or all four modalities to learn.

After we use our learning style to take in information, our brain processes and stores the information with either the left side (left hemisphere) of the brain or the right side (right hemisphere). Each side has a different way of thinking and looking at the world. Some of us have a **left brain hemispheric preference,** some have a **right brain hemispheric preference,** while some use both sides of the brain. **Left-brain learners** tend to be sequential and process information in a linear manner. **Right-brain learners** tend to think globally, seeing the big picture, and connecting seemingly unrelated ideas. Also, left-brain learners think more in symbols such as letters, words, and numbers, while right-brain learners think more in sensory images of sight, sounds, smell, tastes, and touch, and movement, without words.

By determining your learning style and your brain hemispheric preference you can find your superlink—your fastest way of learning. There are eight superlinks to accelerated learning: **visual left-brain, visual right-brain, auditory left-brain, auditory right-brain, tactile left-brain, tactile right-brain, kinesthetic left-brain,** and **kinesthetic right-brain.** The quizzes in the next two chapters will help you find your superlink.

When someone is instructing us in a different way than the one that matches our best style, it is uncomfortable, unnatural, and stressful, and we do not learn as effectively and quickly. For example, think about the hand you use for writing. You have become so used to using that hand that this has become automatic; you do not even think about it. But if you were asked to write with the opposite hand it would be difficult, awkward, slower, and uncomfortable. You could *force* yourself to use that hand, but it would be a struggle. You would be so busy concentrating on getting your hand to write that you might not even be able to focus on what it is you are supposed to be writing. It is the same with our learning style. When we learn through our superlink, learning is easy, effortless, and automatic. When we learn through a learning link that is not easy for us, learning becomes a struggle. Simple? Read on.

The Many Benefits of Knowing Your Best Learning Link

Improving Your Ability to Learn, Study, and Take Tests

By discovering your best learning link you will know how to learn, read, and study more effectively. You will comprehend reading material better and improve your memory, making your study time more productive. Those who have used these techniques have drastically improved their scores on tests—whether for school, entrance examinations, college boards, certifications, or qualifying tests.

Improving Your Communication and Relationships With Others

Not only can you learn faster, you will learn how others'_ learning links work, making you a better communicator, trainer, and instructor when you work with, train, or teach others. Have you ever been frustrated because you spent an hour explaining to your children how to do their homework and they still did not get it? Knowledge of the eight superlinks gets your message across effectively. Whether you work in an office, a corporation, a factory, a store, or anywhere else, by identifying others' learning links you will be able to communicate more effectively with your boss, coworkers, employees, and customers, and improve relations with them. You will find a new power to get your message across in a way that others can understand.

It has helped instructors train others in academic and nonacademic subjects such as in learning a job, an art, a hobby, or a sport. For example, instructors at the Michael Jordan Golf Company, Director of Instruction and 1993 PGA Teacher of the Year, Charlie Long, and Golf Instructor and Missouri State Amateur Golf Champion, Maria Long, say, "We have utilized learning styles while giving golf instruction for several years now. As teachers, it was a major source of frustration to give out what we knew was good information, only to see widely varied results with our learners. What we originally passed off as greater or lesser degrees of talent in our students we now recognize was due to the fact that we did not always give the information in our students' best way of receiving it. We now adapt our approach to the learner—a golf lesson can be a lengthy video viewing session; a richly detailed conversation; a "hands-on" walk through a new motion; or just a super-visual coaching session with short "do" instructions. We have greater peace of mind, and our students obviously love their progress. We feel that adapting to the student's learning style is maybe the real future of golf instruction. We know more than enough ways to swing—we just need better ways to help others understand." Their application to the future of golf instruction holds equally true for instruction in all fields.

Small differences in communication due to various learning styles can stress even the closest relationship. Understanding how you and other individuals learn best can also greatly improve your personal relationships and communication with the "significant others" in your life.

How to Discover Your Best Learning Link

The method for discovering your best learning link is simple. You can have fun using it, and you may also find that it transforms certain aspects of your life.

Let's begin by finding your superlink, which is a combination of your learning style preference and brain hemispheric preference. In the next two chapters are two simple assessments you need to take before reading the rest of the book. One assessment identifies your learning style preference and the other identifies your brain hemispheric preference. You then combine the information from those two tests to find out which of the eight superlinks enables you to learn quickly. You will then be able to apply your superlink's methods for accelerated learning to any subject.

How to Use This Book

This book is almost like eight books in one—one for each of the eight superlinks. You can read the whole book cover to cover, in order, or read only those sections that relate to your superlink, skipping the descriptions and strategies that do not relate to you. After you understand how to accelerate learning through your own superlink you may want to go back and read through the book again to learn how people with other superlinks think and learn.

Get a pen or pencil and paper (or you can write in the book) to start the quizzes in chapters 1 and 2. Then sit back and relax in a comfortable place where you can think without being disturbed, and have fun!

Part 1

Finding Your Superlink to Learning

1

Your Learning Style

In this chapter you will take the learning style preference assessment to find your learning style preference. I am not going to tell you anything about the learning style preferences until the chapters *after* you take these quizzes, because I do not want to color your answers or let you answer in a way that favors the learning style you think you are. In order for this method to work, you have to be as accurate as possible in answering the questions to determine your learning style preference. If you do not answer these accurately and the results indicate that you are a different learning style than what you really are, you will not be learning in your most effective way. For each learning style there are different methods to use, and it would be ineffective for you to use the wrong technique. So be as accurate as you can—as painful as it may be for some!

The key to answering the questions is to select answers or choices that are most natural and comfortable. Although we may be able to behave in ways described in other choices—and we often have to do that on the job or in other situations—one choice will probably feel best to us if left to our own devices. Just as we can force ourselves to write with our nondominant hand, we may also force ourselves to behave in two, three, or four different ways (described in each question) depending on the circumstance. The question to ask yourself is, "Which way feels best and is the least stressful?" It is in this spirit that you should respond to the questions.

What happens if you truly feel you can select more than one choice? For some questions, you may know absolutely that two or three choices (or even all the choices, for some people) are equally true for you. In that case, go ahead and select all those that equally describe you. First try to settle on one choice, and if you are sure that there is more than one best answer, then select the others also.

The Learning Style Preference Assessment

1. When you meet a new person what do you first notice about him or her?
   a. what he or she looks like and how he or she dresses
   b. how the person talks, what he or she says, or his or her voice
   c. how you feel about the person
   d. how the person acts or what he or she does

2. Days after you meet a new person, what do you remember the most about that person?
   a. the person's face
   b. the person's name
   c. how you felt being with the person even though you may have forgotten the name or face
   d. what you and the person did together even though you may have forgotten the name or face

3. When you enter a new room, what do you notice the most?
   a. how the room looks
   b. the sounds or discussion in the room
   c. how comfortable you feel emotionally or physically in the room
   d. what activities are going on and what you can do in the room

4. When you learn something new, which way do you need to learn it?
   a. A teacher gives you something to read on paper or on the board and shows you books, pictures, charts, maps, graphs, or objects, but there is no talking, discussion, or writing.
   b. The teacher explains everything by talking or lecturing and allows you to discuss the topic and ask questions, but does not give you anything to look at, read, write, or do.
   c. The teacher lets you write or draw the information, touch hands-on materials, type on a keyboard, or make something with your hands.
   d. The teacher allows you to get up to do projects, simulations, experiments, play games, role-play, act out real-life situations, explore, make discoveries, or do activities that allow you to move around to learn.

5. When you teach something to others, which of the following do you do?
   a. You give them something to look at like an object, picture or chart, with little or no verbal explanation or discussion.
   b. You explain it by talking, but do not give them any visual materials.
   c. You draw or write it out for them or use your hands to explain.
   d. You demonstrate by doing it and have them do it with you.

6. What type of books do you prefer to read?
   a. books that contain descriptions to help you see what is happening
   b. books containing factual information, history, or a lot of dialogue
   c. books about characters' feelings and emotions, self-help books, books about emotions and relationships, or books on improving your mind or body
   d. short books with a lot of action, or books that help you excel at a sport, hobby, or talent

7. Which of the following activities would you prefer to do in your free time?
   a. read a book or look at a magazine
   b. listen to an audiotaped book, a radio talk show, or listen to or perform music
   c. write, draw, type, or make something with your hands
   d. do sports, build something, or play a game using body movement

8. Which of the following describes how you can read or study best?
   a. You can study with music, noise, or talking going on, because you tune it out.
   b. You cannot study with music, noise or talking going on because you cannot tune it out.
   c. You need to be comfortable, stretched out, and can work with or without music, but negative feelings of others distract you.
   d. You need to be comfortable, stretched out, and can work with or without music, but activity or movement in the room distracts you.

9. When you talk with someone, which way do your eyes move? (You can ask someone to observe you to help you answer this question.)
   a. You need to look directly at the face of the person who is talking to you, and you need that person to look at your face when you talk.
   b. You look at the person only for a short time, and then your eyes move from side to side, left and right.
   c. You only look at the person for a short time to see his or her expression, then you look down or away.
   d. You seldom look at the person and mostly look down or away, but if there is movement or activity, you look in the direction of the activity.

10. Which of the following describes you best?
    a. You notice colors, shapes, designs, and patterns wherever you go and have a good eye for color and design.

b. You cannot stand silence, and when it is too quiet in a place you hum, sing, talk aloud, or turn on the radio, television, audiotapes, or CD's to keep an auditory stimulus in the environment.

c. You are sensitive to people's feelings, your own feelings get hurt easily, you cannot concentrate when others do not like you, and you need to feel loved and accepted in order to work.

d. You have a hard time sitting still in your seat and need to move a lot, and if you do have to sit you will slouch, shift around, tap your feet, or kick or wiggle your legs a lot.

11. Which of the following describes you the best?
   a. You notice when people's clothes do not match or their hair is out of place and often want them to fix it.
   b. You are bothered when someone does not speak well and are sensitive to the sounds of dripping faucets or equipment noise.
   c. You cry at the sad parts of movies or books.
   d. You are restless and uncomfortable when forced to sit still and cannot stay in one place too long.

12. What bothers you the most?
   a. a messy, disorganized place
   b. a place that is too quiet
   c. a place that is not comfortable physically or emotionally
   d. a place where there is no activity allowed or no room to move

13. What bothers you the most when someone is teaching you?
   a. listening to a lecture without any visuals to look at
   b. having to read silently with no verbal explanation or discussion
   c. not being allowed to draw, doodle, touch anything with your hands, or take written notes, even if you never look at your notes again
   d. having to look and listen without being allowed to move

14. Think back to a happy memory from your life. Take a moment to remember as much as you can about the incident. After reliving it, what memories stand out in your mind?
    a. what you saw, such as visual descriptions of people, places, and things
    b. what you heard, such as dialogue and conversation, what you said, and the sounds around you
    c. sensation on your skin and body and how you felt physically and emotionally
    d. what actions and activities you did, the movements of your body, and your performance

15. Recall a vacation or trip you took. For a few moments remember as much as you can about the experience. After reliving the incident, what memories stand out in your mind?
    a. what you saw, such as visual descriptions of people, places, and things
    b. what you heard, such as dialogue and conversation, what you said, and the sounds around you
    c. sensation on your skin and body and how you felt physically and emotionally
    d. what actions and activities you did, the movements of your body, and your performance

16. Pretend you have to spend all your time in one of the following places where different activities are going on. In which one would you feel the most comfortable?
    a. a place where you can read; look at pictures, art work, maps, charts, and photographs; do visual puzzles such as mazes, or find the missing portion of a picture; play word games such as Scrabble or Boggle; do interior decoration, or get dressed up
    b. a place where you can listen to audiotaped stories, music, radio or television talk shows or news; play an instrument or sing; play word games out loud, debate, or pretend to be a disc jockey; read aloud or recite speeches or parts from a play or movie, or read poetry or stories aloud
    c. a place where you can draw, paint, sculpt, or make crafts; do creative writing or type on a computer; do ac-

tivities that involve your hands, such as playing an instrument, games such as chess, checkers, or board games, or build models

d. a place where you can do sports, play ball or action games that involve moving your body, or act out parts in a play or show; do projects in which you can get up and move around; do experiments or explore and discover new things; build things or put together mechanical things; or participate in competitive team activities

17. If you had to remember a new word, would you remember it best by:
    a. seeing it
    b. hearing it
    c. writing it
    d. mentally or physically acting out the word

Scoring Instructions

Total the scores from the assessment as follows (if you gave more than one answer for any question, include all of the choices in the total for each letter):

Add up all the answers marked a and write the total: ____ .
Add up all the answers marked b and write the total: ____ .
Add up all the answers marked c and write the total: ____ .
Add up all the answers marked d and write the total: ____ .

If the a category is your highest score, you are a visual learner. If the b category is your highest score you are an auditory learner. If the c category is your highest score, you are a tactile learner. If the d category is your highest score, you are a kinesthetic learner. Also note your second, third, and least preferred learning style. (Note: Some people have developed several or all learning styles, and two, three, or four learning styles may be tied.)

Write your learning style below so you can refer to it as you proceed through the rest of the book.

My preferred learning style is: _____ .

2

Your Brain Hemispheric Preference

In this chapter you will be taking the brain hemispheric preference assessment to find out which brain hemisphere you prefer to use for understanding and storing new information. Just as in the learning style preference assessment, you will be selecting the choice that is most natural and comfortable for you.

If you are absolutely sure that both answers equally describe you, then select both. Make sure you do not choose both to take the easy way out and rush through the assessment. If you have to choose both answers, do it because you have given it full consideration and are certain that both describe you equally well.

The Brain Hemispheric Preference Assessment

1. Close your eyes. See red. What do you see?
   a. the letters *r-e-d* or nothing because you could not visualize it
   b. the color red or a red object
2. Close your eyes. See three. What do you see?

    a. the letters *t-h-r-e-e,* or the number 3, or perhaps nothing because you could not visualize it

    b. three animals, people, or objects

3. If you play music or sing:
   a. you cannot play by ear and must read notes.
   b. you can play by ear if you need to.

4. When you put something together:
   a. you need to read and follow written directions.
   b. you can use pictures and diagrams or just jump in and do it without using directions.

5. When someone is talking to you:
   a. you pay more attention to words and tune out their nonverbal communication.
   b. you pay more attention to nonverbal communication, such as facial expressions, body language, and tones of voice.

6. You are better at:
   a. working with letters, numbers, and words.
   b. working with color, shapes, pictures, and objects.

7. When you read fiction, do you:
   a. hear the words being read aloud in your head?
   b. see the book played as a movie in your head?

8. Which hand do you write with?
   a. right hand
   b. left hand

9. When doing a math problem, which way is easiest for you?
   a. to work it out in the form of numbers and words
   b. to draw it out, work it out using hands-on materials, or use your fingers

10. Do you prefer to:
    a. talk about your ideas?
    b. do something with real objects?

11. How do you keep your room or your desk?
    a. neat and organized

  b. messy or disorganized to others, but you know where everything is

12. If no one is telling you what to do, which is more like you?
  a. You do things on a schedule and stick to it.
  b. You do things at the last minute or in your own time, and/or want to keep working even when time is up.

13. If no one were telling you what to do:
  a. you would usually be on time.
  b. you would often be late.

14. You like to read a book or magazine:
  a. from front to back.
  b. from back to front or by skipping around.

15. Which describes you best?
  a. You like to tell and hear about events with all the details told in order.
  b. You like to tell the main point of an event, and when others are telling you about an event you get restless if they do not get to the main idea quickly.

16. When you do a puzzle or project, do you:
  a. do it well without seeing the finished product first?
  b. need to see the finished product before you can do it?

17. Which method of organizing notes do you like best:
  a. outlining or listing things in order
  b. making a mind map, or web, with connected circles

18. When you are given instructions to make something, if given the choice, would you:
  a. prefer to follow the instructions?
  b. prefer to think of new ways to do it and try it a different way?

19. When you sit at a desk, do you:
  a. sit up straight?
  b. slouch or lean over your desk, lean back in your chair to be comfortable, or stay partly out of the seat?

20. Which describes you best?

    a. You spell words and write numbers correctly most of the time.

    b. You sometimes mix up letters or numbers or write some words, letters, or numbers in reverse order or backward.

21. Which is more like you?

    a. You speak words correctly and in the right order.

    b. You sometimes mix up words in a sentence or say a different one than what you mean, but you know what you mean.

22. You usually:

    a. stick to a topic when talking to people.

    b. change the topic to something else you thought of related to it.

23. You like to:

    a. make plans and stick to them.

    b. decide things at the last minute, go with the flow, or do what you feel like at the moment.

24. You like to do:

    a. art projects in which you follow directions or step-by-step instructions.

    b. art projects that give you freedom to create what you want.

25. You like:

    a. to play music or sing based on written music or what you learned from others.

    b. create your own music, tunes, or songs.

26. You like:

    a. sports that have step-by-step instructions or rules.

    b. sports that allow you to move freely without rules.

27. You like to:

    a. work step-by-step, in order, until you get to the end product.

    b. see the whole picture or end product first and then go back and work the steps.

28. Which describes you the best?
    a. You think about facts and events that really happened.
    b. You think in an imaginative and inventive way about what could happen or what could be created in the future.

29. You know things because:
    a. you learn from the world, other people, or reading.
    b. you know them intuitively, and you can't explain how or why you know.

30. You like to:
    a. stick to facts.
    b. imagine what could be.

31. You usually:
    a. keep track of time.
    b. lose track of time.

32. You are:
    a. good at reading nonverbal communication.
    b. not good at reading nonverbal communication.

33. You are:
    a. better at directions given verbally or in writing.
    b. better at directions given with pictures or maps4

34. You are better at:
    a. being creative with existing materials and putting them together in a new way.
    b. inventing or producing what is new and never existed.

35. You usually work on:
    a. one project at a time, in order.
    b. many projects at the same time.

36. In which of the following environments would you prefer to work?
    a. a structured environment where everything is orderly, some-one is telling you what to do, a time schedule is kept, and you do one project at a time, step-by-step, and in order.

b. an unstructured environment where you have freedom of choice and movement to work on what you want, where you can be as creative and imaginative as you want, keep your belongings any way you want, and do as many projects as you wish simultaneously, without any set time schedule.

Scoring Instructions

Score 1 point for each question you answered with only a and write the total: _____

Score 1 point for each question you answered with only b and write the total: _____

Score 1 point for each question you answered both a and b (tied score) and write the total: _____

If your highest score is in category a, you show a preference for using the left hemisphere of the brain.

If your highest score is in category b, you show a preference for using the right hemisphere of the brain.

If your highest score is in the "tied" category, you show an integrated use of both sides of the brain.

If you had almost the same number of checks for a and b (not including the tied column), then you may have a mixed preference and are using each side of the brain for different functions. If there are one or two more checks in either side a or b, then you have a mixed preference favoring the right hemisphere or a mixed preference favoring the left.

Write your preferred brain hemispheric preference here:

_____ .

(Choices are: left, right, integrated (tied), mixed preference, mixed preference favoring the right hemisphere, mixed preference favoring the left hemisphere.)

3

Your Superlink

After taking the learning style preference assessment and the brain hemispheric preference assessment you can combine the results to find your superlink.

Since the 1980s, when I began using learning styles and brain hemispheric preferences to teach students, I realized there was a difference between those who were visual learners with a right-brain preference and those who were visual learners with a left-brain preference. Similarly, there were auditory learners with a right-brain preference and some with a left-brain preference, and the way these two groups learned differed vastly. While teachers who used learning styles would only assess whether their students were visual, auditory, tactile, or kinesthetic, and those who assessed brain hemispheric preference would only concentrate on the differences between the right and left sides of the brain, I had not found any system that combined the two. For years, I always looked at the whole picture—learning style and brain hemispheric preference combined. Working closely with a large range of learners, in case after case I saw that both assessments had to be taken into account in order to accelerate one's learning. Thus, I found there were eight broad categories and a vast difference between the way each group learned. I have named these the eight superlinks to accelerated learning because they provide the fastest and most effective link between the material to be learned and our brain. The word *superlink* is used to make a distinction between this combined method and the use of only visual, auditory, tactile, or kinesthetic learning styles. Since the term *learning style,* used by most people, excludes brain hemispheric dominance, I have coined the term *superlink* because this includes both our learning style preference and our brain hemispheric preference.

How to Find Your Superlink

You will now take the results of both assessments, the learning style preference assessment and the brain hemispheric preference assessment, to find your own superlink to learning. Take your learning style from page 10 and your brain hemispheric preference and combine them to form your superlink. Here are the possible combinations that can result:

visual left-brain   visual right-brain
auditory left-brain   auditory right-brain
tactile left-brain   tactile right-brain
kinesthetic left-brain   kinesthetic right-brain

The above are the eight superlinks to accelerated learning.

Write your superlink here: _____

Superlink Combinations

There are also people who may use a combination of these eight superlinks. If your brain hemispheric preference is integrated, your possible superlinks are:

visual right-and-left-brain integrated
auditory right-and-left-brain integrated
tactile right-and-left-brain integrated
kinesthetic right-and-left-brain integrated

The possible combinations of superlinks for mixed prefer-ences are:

visual right-and-left-brain mixed preference
auditory right-and-left-brain mixed preference
tactile right-and-left-brain mixed preference
kinesthetic right-and-left-brain mixed preference

You may also use a combination of learning styles. Some people can be visual and auditory; others can be tactile and au-ditory. Some use two, three, or all four learning styles equally; others use all four learning styles and have an integrated prefer-ence for both sides of the brain—this person would be using his or her *whole* brain.

The following chapters contain descriptions of each type of learner and the key to learning rapidly. You will understand what each learning style preference and brain hemispheric preference means for you, and how your superlink to accelerated learning can help you learn better.

Part 2

Learning Styles and Brain Hemispheric Preferences

4

What Is a Learning Style?

You have taken the learning style preference assessment and know what your best learning style is. Now you will learn what it means to have the learning style you do.

Our learning style is one part of our superlink to accelerated learning. Research has identified that people learn in different ways. We rely on all our senses to receive information from the outside world, yet, over time, many people develop one sense more than others and find it easier to rely on that one for learning new material. This is how we develop a preference for one type of learning style. If we want to learn something rapidly, the material needs to be presented to us in our most developed pathway to the brain—our learning style. There are four main learning styles: visual, auditory, tactile, and kinesthetic.

Visual learners learn by seeing.

Auditory learners learn by listening, hearing themselves talk, and discussing their thoughts with others.

Tactile learners learn by touching or feeling sensation on their skin, by using their hands and fingers, and connecting what they learn to their sense of touch or their emotions.

Kinesthetic learners learn by moving their large, or gross, muscles in space, and by getting actively involved in the learning process through simulations, role-play, experimentation, exploration, and movement, and participating in real-life activities.

Learners who use other senses: Though they are rare, there are also some learners who rely on their sense of taste and touch. Although they are not addressed in the assessment, these learners have an acute sense of smell or taste, are sensitive to odors or tastes, and can learn well by involving these senses.

Learning Style and the Brain

Brain research has advanced enough that we have at least a *limited* understanding of how the brain works. Although there is still much to learn, we do know some basic principles that are relevant to understanding how we learn. As our brains are exposed to stimuli, new interconnections between nerve cells are created; this quality is known as plasticity. The more stimuli we receive, the more interconnections and learning patterns are formed. Thus, as certain learning patterns become more rapid, easier, and automatic, we learn more quickly, developing our best learning style. This is the essence of accelerated learning.

We have pathways between our senses and our brains. If, over time, we have relied more upon our eyes, then the passageways between the nerves in our eyes and the part of the brain that interprets visual stimuli were developed more than passageways between the brain and other senses. As a result, we find it easier to rely upon our eyes. For some people, the neural connections between the ears and the part of the brain that interprets auditory stimuli are stronger; thus, they find it easier and quicker to learn through the ears. For others the neural passageways between the skin, hands, and fingers and the part of the brain that interprets tactile stimuli of feeling physical sensation and physical responses to emotion has been used more and those people find it easier to learn though the sense of touch. Some have made more use of their large motor muscles, so the neural pathways from their muscles to the part of the brain that senses body motion have become stronger. Thus, we have people with increased ability to learn kinesthetically.

When learning something new, we need to concentrate on assimilating the new information, process, or skill. We do not want to be encumbered by trying to learn through a weak sensory modality, so to accelerate learning, new information should be presented in our best learning style. If you want to develop other learning styles, you can do so when you are *not* trying to learn new material. The basic rule of thumb is: If you want to learn something quickly, learn it through your preferred learning style.

How Learning Styles Develop

Learning styles are a combination of nature and nurture. Some tendencies are genetically inherited, some are a result of exposure to certain stimuli over a long period of time, and some develop due to one's reliance on that particular sense for survival. These repeated stimuli strengthen certain passageways between one or more senses and the brain.

There are men and women who fall into each of the learning style categories. There are visual men and visual women. Similarly, there are auditory men and auditory women, tactile men and tactile women, kinesthetic men and kinesthetic women. While certain learning styles—like the kinesthetic, or movement-oriented learning style—seem to be attributed in our society more to men, and others—like the tactile, or emotionally-oriented learning style—seem to be attributed more to women, these stereotypes do not hold true in reality. Cultural pressures may have influenced numbers of each gender to exhibit certain behaviors. As a result, people may have been forced to suppress their natural way of learning to conform to social expectations. However, over the past decade people of both genders have been given more opportunities to engage in a wider range of experiences, allowing them to develop along the lines of their natural way of learning. Thus, we find people of both sexes developing all of the learning styles. I hope that, with this newfound knowledge of learning styles, parents and teachers will realize the importance of exposing the young to stimuli that develop *all* their senses, giving them an opportunity to develop their *whole* brain and make better use of their natural talents.

A question frequently raised is: Since traditional schools teach people mostly through the visual and auditory senses, wouldn't all learners develop into visual and auditory learners? The answer can best be understood by a similar question: If you are right-handed, would you become left-handed if you were forced to use only the left hand in school? Think of what that would be like. You could *force* yourself to use your left hand but you would be slower, more conscious of the motions of writing than the actual work, and it might take you years to become as proficient with your left hand as you are with your right. (The same situation would be applicable if we were to make left-handed people write with their right hand. It may take you the same number of years to develop your nondominant hand as it took to become automatic with your dominant hand, putting you several years back in development of skills that require writing ability. Similarly, if you were a visual, tactile, or kinesthetic learner you could force yourself to develop your auditory sense, but during the years you are developing it you would struggle with material presented auditorily, putting you at a disadvantage in that environment. The same holds true for forcing auditory, tactile, or kinesthetic learners into a visual environment. When learning something new, you naturally want to use your most comfortable sense to accelerate progress. At other times you can strengthen your weaker senses, and over time they will become stronger, but they will not equal your ability in your strongest sense unless you stop using it for a part of that time.

The Four Types of Learners

While each learner is unique, people who have the same learning style share some similar characteristics. In the following chapters on the eight superlinks, each learning style will be described so you can understand yourself and others.

You may want to begin with the chapter on your own learning style first, and then read the descriptions of the other types.

If you scored equally in several learning styles, read descriptions of those two, three, or possibly four. Highlight the characteristics in each that describe your personal profile. You may also recognize qualities of other people you know.

You may find that most characteristics describe you, or only some. If the latter is true, the descriptions may not match you completely because you use a mixture of two or more learning styles. Although we may be strong in one learning style, this does not mean we neglect to use others in different situations. Thus you will have to read the characteristics of each to see which portions apply to you, though the description may not match completely if you did not answer the assessment accurately. It could be that in our jobs we develop other senses, and in taking the questionnaire we were identifying with our work persona. If that is the case, you may find that you have several learning styles—your work style, your style when dealing with other people, and the style you are at heart.

The chart on the following pages show some of the general differences between visual, auditory, tactile, and kinesthetic learners. These descriptions are not meant to be a system for labeling people for all time; rather, they allow us to form a profile of ourselves, and help us communicate better and learn more easily and rapidly. Chapters 10 to 17 on the eight superlinks fully describe the combination of learning style with brain hemispheric preference and its application to accelerated learning.

Distinguishing Characteristics	Visual Learners	Auditory Learners	Tactile Learners	Kinesthetic Learners
Receiving Information	seeing, using visual aids or watching live demonstrations	hearing, speaking, reading aloud, discussing or processing thoughts aloud	sensation on the skin, sense of touch, use of hands and fingers, feeling (physically or emotionally)	movement of large motor muscles, involvement in movement activities, exploration, learning while body is in motion
Sensitivity to Environment	sensitive to visual environment; need attractive surroundings; distracted by visual disorganization	need continual auditory stimuli, and when it is silent will make own sounds by humming, singing, whistling, or talking to oneself, except when studying, when silence is required, or to tune out auditory distractions of others	sensitive to physical sensation, one's own and other people's feelings; aware of nonverbal communication such as facial expressions, body language, and tones of voice; read other's feelings louder than their words; cannot tune out the negativity and feelings of others to concentrate on work	attuned to movement and action in the environment; need space to move about; attention is attracted by movement; distracted by movement of others, although needs to move in order to learn
What is noticed when meeting someone new	a person's face, clothes, and appearance	a person's name, the sound of the voice, the way someone talks, and what the person says	how they feel being with the other person	how he or she acts; what the other person does; and what they did together

Eye movement (Note: The descriptions of eye movements are generally true for each of the learning styles, but there are numerous exceptions due to cultural, sociological, family influences, and personality traits. New research is investigating different eye movements related to when we use long- and short-term memory as well.)	when thinking, tend to look up towards the ceiling; when listening, need eye contact with the speaker and want those listening to them to make eye contact as well	tend to look left and right in the direction of their ears with only brief eye contact with the speaker	tend to look at others to read their facial expressions and body language, but listen best when their eyes are down and away, the eye position for processing at an emotional level	listen and think best when eyes are down and away, with little eye contact, because that is the position for connecting learning with movement, but if there is activity in the surroundings, their eyes go in the direction of the activity
Speech	describe visual elements such as color, shape, size, and how things look	describe sound, voice, music, sound effects, and noise in the environment, and recount what people say	describe bodily comfort, physical sensation, and emotions; express themselves with hand movements and nonverbal communication	use action words; talk about doing, winning, and achieving; generally speak few words and get to the point; may use body to act out movements while speaking
Memory	good memory for visual surroundings and what was seen in print or in graphics	good memory for dialogue, music, and sound	good memory for events tied to feelings and physical sensation, and what was done with the hands	good memory for action and movements

5

What Is Brain Hemispheric Preference?

The brain is divided into two hemispheres, or halves—the right and the left. While we all use both sides of the brain, many people process and store information using one side more than the other, exhibiting a **brain hemispheric preference.** A preference for one side of the brain develops when we use particular neural pathways more, developing them to a higher degree; we become more skilled in using that hemisphere. It is not that we are incapable of using the other side of the brain, but when we use one half more, over time it feels more comfortable and natural to use.

When people receive instruction in a way that does not match their brain hemispheric preference they may take longer to learn, they may struggle, or even fail. But when we communicate in the way that matches our brain hemispheric preference, we learn more easily and quickly.

Scientists have helped us understand some of the characteristics of the right and left sides of the brain. Each side looks at life differently. Thus, someone who processes mostly through the right side of the brain will experience an event or situation differently from one who processes mostly through the left side of the brain.

Our brain hemispheric preference is not a conscious choice, but we grow up mostly using one side for many tasks. As children we may have been exposed to many linear tasks, so our brain had enough stimuli to develop neural pathways that support left-brain thinking. Or, we may have been exposed to many wholistic and global experiences, stimulating the development of right-brain thinking.

Neither side of the brain is superior to the other; they merely do different tasks important for survival. Ideally, people should be able to use both sides of their brains equally well. Unfortunately, this information on brain hemispheric preference has only recently become public knowledge. Left to chance, people often end up using one side more than the other and rely on that side for all tasks, even those more appropriately handled by the other side. This is why many people have difficulty learning or find it takes them a long time to learn. While we are waiting for the educational system to catch up and use the new teaching methods that engage both hemispheres of the brain, we need to find ways to deal with the limitations we inherited. Thus, if you have favored one side of the brain for most tasks, you will learn techniques to adapt any learning situation to be compatible with your brain preference.

Can we develop the other side of our brain if we have a preference? Yes, we can, but it takes time. Everyone has spent a certain number of years learning through one side of the brain, and you can calculate how long it may take to balance that by developing the other side. In the meantime, if you have a preference, you can use it to your advantage to accelerate learning by having material presented to you in a way that is compatible with the way your brain works. The rule is: Learn something new through your preferred side. When not learning, develop the undeveloped side of the brain.

While scientists are still mapping the brain and have not yet completed work that will give us a full understanding of how the entire brain works, we currently know a great deal and can apply these findings to the field of accelerated learning.

Learning Style and Brain Hemispheric Preference

Learning style relates to the different ways of receiving material from the world and conveying those messages from the senses to the brain. Brain hemispheric preference deals with what we do with the data—how we process, or think about it, and store it once it reaches the brain.

The sensory data received from our eyes, ears, sense of touch, or the muscles of our body can be channeled to the right or left side of the brain. These process and store the information in different ways. It is essential to know these differences to learn anything quickly.

Some educators focus only on using learning styles when teaching, while others focus only on using brain hemispheric preference. To have a total picture of the way people need to learn, a blending of both is required; thus, the development of the concept of a superlink: learning style *plus* brain hemispheric preference. It is necessary to know our best learning style and our brain hemispheric preference to accelerate learning.

Differences Between the Left and Right Hemispheres

Processing Information: Symbolically versus Sensorially

One difference in the way the sides of the brain process is that the left side processes data symbolically in the form of letters, numbers, words, and abstract ideas, and the right side processes data in a sensory way, perceiving the world through the senses, without words.

The left hemisphere allows human beings to have the gift of language. Without it, we would only perceive what we see, hear, taste, smell, and touch, and our movements—without words. We would not be able to talk about our experiences or communicate them to others. In most people, the left side of the brain handles language, although there are exceptions: One report states that in five percent of right-handed people and thirty percent of left-handed people, the speech area is in the right hemisphere of the brain.[1] Think of the hemisphere in which our speech and language center is located as a built-in translator that takes whatever happens and puts words or numbers to it.

The right side of the brain processes information without language. It perceives sensations of sight, touch, smell, taste, movement, music, the sounds of the human voice and of nature without putting words or labels to the experience. It perceives life as a movie without words.

Although everyone processes language, the difference is that some people first process everything into words and language, while other people first perceive the event as a pure sensory experience without words. As the material is processed in someone's mind, they can "think" about it either in words, as if a dialogue were going on in their head, or can "think" about it in sensory images full of sight, sound, smell, taste, and touch, as well as movement, without words. If you wonder how this is possible, think of a time when you saw someone you knew but could not remember his or her name. You tried so hard to remember but drew a blank—yet you were sure you knew the person. This is an example of how the right brain functions—without words.

This information is critical in terms of accelerated learning. Why? If someone processes information in symbols such as words, he or she will respond to being taught in terms of words and language. If someone processes information in sensory images, he or she will respond to being taught in terms of sensory images and experiences. When we match the presentation of new material to our brain hemispheric preference, learning is assured.

[1]From *The Brain: A Neuroscience Primer,* 2nd ed., by Richard F. Thompson (New York: W. H. Freeman and Co., 1993), 397.

When we do not do this, we struggle with learning new material and may not understand the material at all.

This does not mean that none of us use both sides of the brain to process information. Everyone is capable of speaking and receiving sensory images; we blend the two together to learn and to perform different tasks. The difference is that when we are learning something new for the first time we tend to process the new material through our preferred brain hemisphere. If we receive data through our preferred side of the brain it is more automatic, natural, and easier for us to accelerate our learning.

Storing Information: Step-by-Step or Simultaneously

When we learn something new, we also find it easier if the material is presented in a way that matches the way we *store* information. The left side of the brain stores it in a sequential, step-by-step order. The left side absorbs information in a linear order, bit by bit, one piece at a time. It has difficulty getting the big picture unless information is presented sequentially. The right side of the brain stores information in a simultaneous, global way; it sees the whole picture at once. It has difficulty receiving information in a step-by-step way unless it gets the big picture. Both sides of the brain are equally important, have their role to play in human life, and must work together.

Are there people who can store information both ways? Yes. These people have developed the use of both sides of the brain. They are equally comfortable with both left-brain linear thinking and right-brain global thinking. Those who do not use both sides of the brain, who favor one side, need to know their preference in order to find out how to learn more rapidly.

The characteristics of both sides of the brain will be described in the chapters on the eight superlinks. Keep in mind that few people use only one side exclusively. Thus, few people have *all* of the characteristics described for either right-brain or left-brain learners. The higher your score for a left-brain preference, the closer you come to the description of the left-brain characteristics. The higher your score for a right-brain preference, the closer you will be to the description of the characteristics of the right-brain learner.

On the quiz, if you had tied scores for right-brain and left-brain functions, or mixed preference in which you used the right brain for certain tasks and the left brain for others, then in the section on the eight superlinks you will need the chapters on left-brain learners and right-brain learners because you have characteristics of both. For example, if you are kinesthetic with integrated use of both sides of the brain, read the chapters on the kinesthetic left-brain learner and kinesthetic right-brain learner. If you are a visual learner with a mixed preference, read the chapters on the visual left-brain learner and the visual right-brain learner, and for your individual profile, highlight the aspects of each side of the brain that apply to you.

If you use both sides of the brain equally, also read Chapter 6, which describes the integrated use of both sides of the brain. If you were right-brain for certain tasks and left-brain for others, refer to Chapter 7 for a description of the characteristics of having a mixed preference. This data is important because you are identifying how you need to learn. In the later chapters you will be applying this information in ways to learn any subject quickly.

The following chart gives a summary of what is currently known so far about the two hemispheres of the brain.

Although intuition has been traditionally assigned to the right side of the brain, research has not confirmed this. What is perceived as intuition could actually be a function of reading nonverbal communication, synthesizing unrelated material and events into a whole, or using imagination or inventiveness. Both right-brain and left-brain people may have intuition. Future studies may reveal that intuition may be beyond the scope of the right or left hemispheres of the brain.

Each year we discover new things about the brain. As new studies arise, current data is subject to change. We must continually revise our existing knowledge as these new findings arise.

Left Hemisphere	Right Hemisphere
Controls movement of the right side of the body: right hand, right foot, etc.	Controls movement of the left side of the body: left hand, left foot, etc.
Receives sensory and tactile input from the right side of the body, including the right hand	Receives sensory and tactile input from the left side of the body, including the left hand
Processes symbolic language: letters, numbers, words, language, ideas, concepts	Processes sensory experience that is concrete: sights, sounds, or sensory impressions without words, or with words that have a strong sensory association
Verbal communication	Nonverbal communication: reads facial gestures, body language, tones of voice, and emotional cues
Step-by-step, linear, sequential order	Simultaneous, global, big picture
Temporal: Perceives time order (a function of having a step-by-step, linear, and sequential order)	Nontemporal: not aware of time order (due to lack of a step-by-step, linear, and sequential order)
Analyzes by breaking down into parts	Synthesizes by connecting parts into a whole
Part-to-whole learning	Whole-to-part learning
Poor visual-spatial relationships	Good visual-spatial relationships: arranging blocks, drawing three-dimensional objects, etc.

Left Hemisphere	Right Hemisphere
Listens more to words than emotional overtones	Perceives others' emotions
Music: timing, sequential or linear aspects of music production, analyzing music	Music: playing by ear, wholistic appreciation of music, synthesizing different sounds into a whole
Creative with existing material	Creative by thinking of that which does not yet exist, inventive, imaginative

6

Integrated Right-and-Left-Brain Learners

People who have developed the ability to use both sides of their brain are called integrated right-and-left-brain learners. They use each side appropriately for the task at hand. For tasks that would be more easily accomplished by the right side of the brain, they use right-brain functions. Conversely, for tasks that are easily handled by the left side of the brain, they use the left side. Thus, this group of people learns easily in any kind of environment, a left- or right-brain one.

How to Become Integrated

Those who work in brain research advocate the development of both sides of the brain to make fuller use of our potential. We can continue to increase the capabilities of our brain; it is never too late to work on our weaker side, though to accelerate learning we still want to learn through our preferred side of the brain. However, in those off hours when we are not trying to learn something new, we can engage in activities that stimulate the other side of the brain. Thus, left-brain learners should spend some time, daily, in right-brain activities, and vice versa. You can read through the descriptions of the right-brain visual, auditory, tactile, and kinesthetic learners to find out what activities they do and spend some time in some of them, each day, to develop the right side of your brain. To develop the left brain, read descriptions of the left-brain visual, auditory, tactile, and kinesthetic learners and start doing left-brain activities daily.

Left-brain people can develop the right side of their brains by using their left hands to draw or write, brainstorming, inventing, doing creative writing, reading people's nonverbal expressions such as facial gestures, tones of voice, and body language (turn off the sound on a video to figure out the feelings behind the actors' and actresses' gestures), taking new routes to work, or putting the clock away and working without it for a whole day.

Right-brain people can develop left-brain skills by using their right hands for drawing, writing, or doing activities (if they are not already right-handed). To develop the left brain's sequential, step-by-step abilities, read a story or an article and make a mind map filling in all the details, then convert the mind map into a traditional left-brain outline format in a linear, sequential way, get a file cabinet and file your papers alphabetically or chronologically, get a planning book or calendar and write down your appointments, and set a goal to keep each one on time. Get a watch or beeper and program it to go off as a reminder to keep your appointments, or your to-do list, on time.

The following are characteristics of integrated left-and-right-brain learners.

Understanding the World: Integrated learners can think in terms of symbols and language as well as sensory experiences. When asked to see blue, they may see both the color and the letters that spell the word *blue.* They can remember sensory impressions as they would see a movie in their heads, and can also use words and symbols to think about what they perceived. Their lives are enriched because they can think and process in both symbolic language such as words, symbols, and ideas, and in pictorial language and sensory input. Just as someone who is bilingual can communicate in two languages with a wider range of people, integrated learners can move easily from one environment to another and can understand people and subjects who communicate both in a right-brain and left-brain manner.

Storing Material: Integrated thinkers store information both simultaneously and in a step-by-step way. Thus, they can grasp the big picture in a simultaneous way, and go back and file its details in a sequential way. At times they may work in a wholistic way, thinking about the big picture. At other times, they may organize their ideas or papers in a step-by-step way, alphabetically, numerically, or in some order that makes sense to them. This ability gives them the added advantage of picking the storage system that matches the task.

This flexibility also enables them to learn from both a right-brain, global presentation as well as from a left-brain, step-by-step linear presentation. When they present data they do it in either a simultaneous or step-by-step way.

Sense of Time: Integrated thinkers are aware of time. They can hide out in the right side of the brain and become oblivious of time, or they can be very scheduled when they shift over to attending to the functions of the left side of the brain. Thus, they can also pick and choose whether they will live according to a schedule or become lost in timelessness. With experience they learn which situations require a sense of time and which do not.

Visual-Spatial Relationships: The right side of the brain gives integrated thinkers the ability to deal with visual-spatial relationships with good perception of color, shape, and design. They are aware of the relation of objects and people in space.

Creativity and Imagination: Integrated right-and-left-brain thinkers can deal with two types of creativity. They can work with existing forms and objects or ideas and put them together in new ways, or they can create something new. With full use of their brain, they have a wide range of options open to them.

Communication: Integrated thinkers can "listen" through both sides of the brain. Thus, they are hearing words *and* picking up nonverbal cues as well. This makes them more aware and conscious of what is happening around them than those who only receive information through one side of the brain. Thus, integrated thinkers are attending to the meaning of the words as well as the hidden meaning expressed by the speaker's tone of voice, or facial and body gestures. This ability allows them to communicate in an empathetic way, to speak articulately and couple this with expressive gestures or tones of voice.

Whole-to-Part and Part-to-Whole Thinking: Integrated thinkers can look at information in both ways. They can start with the big picture and then go back and analyze the details, or they can go through the details in a linear way and then understand the sum total at the end. They can look at a book from front to back as well as back to front, or by skipping around, and be equally as happy. This fluidity of thought enables them to function in different types of learning environments with different instructors.

Synthesis vs. Analysis: Integrated people can move comfortably between analyzing and synthesizing. They can break down an idea or process into its component parts and put them back together in the same or a new way. This makes them ideal inventors and creators. They are adept at finding new solutions to problems, creating new gadgets or inventions, finding new ways to create in the arts, or new ways to look at the world. They can look at their new synthesis in an analytical way so they can test it out and examine it for flaws and correct it. These people can see the total synthesis and analyze its parts to ensure that no aspect of a project or product has been left out.

The Downside of Being Integrated

With capabilities on both sides of the brain, the downside of being integrated means that these people may feel there are two people living inside them, each competing for attention. They tend to be so diverse and talented and have so many interests that they are overwhelmed by their own capabilities and find it hard to prioritize. They have so much they want to do, so many people to meet and places to see, that they cannot do all they want to do. They are limited by the number of hours in the day and years in their lives. This creates its own kind of frustration, because with their expanded capabilities there is so much they want to accomplish in so little time.

Benefits of Being Integrated

One of the greatest plusses of having integrated use of both sides of the brain is in the area of discovery, invention, and creation. The right side of the brain can create new art forms, scientific discoveries, and inventions, and the left side has the ability to communicate it to the world through language. There are some people who create something new but do not know how to get it across to others. Thus, it may just live and die with them. But having the ability to put one's creations or inventions into language to help others understand it, or to be able to write it up or speak about it in a sequential, logical way so that others can carry it further or do something with it, is an important quality to have. Thus, those with integrated use of both sides of the brain can make important contributions to humanity that others can understand and use.

7

Right-and-Left-Brain Mixed Preferences

Some people have a right-and-left-brain mixed preference, which means that they perform some functions with one side of the brain and other functions with the other side. When they use the side of the brain that matches the task, there is no problem. Mixed preference learners just need to be aware of their strengths and know how to apply them to the task.

Sometimes people with a mixed preference use one side of the brain, but not necessarily in a way that matches the task. Some people use the right side of the brain for tasks that are better performed by the left side, and vice versa. Thus, these people may find their performance is not always at its best. At worst, it creates confusion and makes learning a great struggle in certain situations. Because of the difficulties this may create, in the rest of this chapter we will focus on the situations in which one is not using his/her brain in the best or most appropriate manner for the task, and what can be done about it.

Using the Right Side of the Brain
for Left-Brain Tasks

Most academic subjects in schools have been based on tasks such as reading, writing, spelling, grammar, public speaking, foreign language, and certain math computation functions that have been traditionally taught in a left-brain way, requiring understanding abstract symbols such as numbers, letters, and words. People who use the right side of the brain when taught in this left-brain manner find that it does not work and end up struggling. One reason these subjects are taught in a left-brain manner is that many people who became teachers and college instructors were people who succeeded in the educational system and could function well in this left-brain environment. Thus, when they taught the upcoming generation, they tended to use the same techniques—left-brain ones—that helped them learn the material. All the subjects listed below can be taught in a right-brain manner so that right-brain people can be successful. Right-brain techniques are presented throughout Part 4 of the book, which gives right-brain strategies for learning anything quickly.

Reading: People with right-brain preferences read differently than those who read with the left side of their brain. The right side of their brain recognizes visual images, words, and patterns they have seen before. Right-brain people learn to read through sight-word recognition or by repeating patterns, known as linguistics or phonemic patterns, in which you read *at*, *fat*, *cat*, *hat*, and so forth. They also respond to sensory words that invoke strong images processed in the right side of the brain. Thus, when they read they are going after the big picture, the main points, the strong visual images, actions, sounds, and feelings. There is nothing wrong with reading in this manner unless you have to attend to details, abstract ideas, or small words that can change the meaning of the text. It also causes difficulties when one has to perform on an important test or task. Even if a right-brain person gets the main idea of what they read they may end up struggling with final examinations, certification tests, qualifying tests, entrance examinations, or tests of reading abilities. They are placed at a disadvantage and low scores may mean anything from failure to low-self-esteem, to not getting admitted into the school of their choice, and sadly, to dropping out. If a right-brain person's career depends on certification it could also affect his or her future. There are two options available to right-brain people who have to perform a left-brain reading task. One is to develop their left-brain skills. The second is to convert the task into a right-brain one so as to perform it well. Without this training, right-brain people may pass through a good portion of their lives needlessly struggling with reading, feeling like failures, and missing many opportunities to advance themselves and their career.

Spelling: Spelling is another task that requires writing letters in order, a left-brain function. Again, those who are using the right side of the brain for spelling will often find themselves mixing up letters because the right brain does not work in sequential order. This means that they may be a good writer, but in school or job situations people will see their poor spelling and may disregard their writing abilities.

Grammar: Poor grammar can reflect on one's writing abilities, speaking abilities, and educational background. A right-brained person could be brilliant, but if he or she does not speak or write grammatically others will not know the depth of his or her intelligence. Again, right-brain students struggle and find themselves getting low scores when it comes to tasks involving grammar even though they may have brilliant ideas, because grammar requires attention to details and sequential order.

Writing: Right-brain people may have great and creative ideas, but much of writing in schools and on the job is evaluated according to left-brain rules and criteria. Thus, organization and logical structure, writing ideas in sequence, correct sentence structure, and correct use of the mechanics of writing are left-brain functions.

Foreign Languages: Foreign language study requires success in reading, writing, spelling, speaking, and grammar. It also requires the storage of two languages in the brain. People who use the right side of the brain to learn a foreign language may find themselves struggling with certain tasks.

Math: Certain math tasks pose another problem for people who use the right side of the brain. Many math problems can be done with right-brain techniques. Right-brain people can grasp the whole picture, identifying a pattern, and see interconnections. But when the task is presented as a word problem or as a problem the reader must solve in a step-by-step method, right-brain people tend to struggle. Even when they can get the right answer for a problem they often do not get credit because they did not write down a detail. They are often penalized for being unable to explain, in words, how they arrived at an answer.

Sometimes people with a strong right-brain preference may transpose numbers. They know what number they are writing, but when they write, two numbers often come out transposed or totally backward. This happens because the right side of the brain sees the whole number simultaneously; it is the left side of the brain that puts the digits in order. When a right-brain person does not take the time to double-check a number it may come out mixed up. Thus, tasks involving accuracy of computation may suffer.

Jobs: There are many jobs that require attention to order and detail: computer programming, accounting, being a bank teller or a cashier, engineering, proofreading, to name a few. People who have a mixed preference should be aware that they will have to use the left side of the brain to perform the tasks listed above.

Right-brain adaptations are given in Part 4 of this book, which focuses on learning with the appropriate side of the brain.

Using the Left Side of the Brain
for Right-Brain Tasks

When someone with a mixed preference has been in the habit of using the left side of the brain to perform right-brain tasks, they may struggle just as do those who use the right side of the brain when performing left-brain tasks. Here are some situations in which using the left brain may impede performance of a right-brain task.

In offices or planning sessions, brainstorming is often a desirable way to generate ideas and solutions for problems. The session requires letting one's mind stay open to various possibilities. It is a time in which suggestions on the floor can trigger other associations and ideas. Someone with a mixed preference may end up engaging the left side of the brain and hindering the brainstorming session. Instead of staying open to all possible suggestions, the left-brainer will begin judging and analyzing each suggestion in a microscopic way, arguing why it would or would not work. The brainstorming session is not the time for judging and evaluating the details of each idea. Interrupting a brainstorming session—a right-brain task—can bog down the process and stop the free flow of ideas needed to find solutions. The left brain needs to reserve its analytical abilities for a later time, after the brainstorming is over, when the specific suggestions are looked at for their practicality.

In tasks such as art, music, new product design, movie production, science and technology, or advertising, which involve creating or inventing something new, left-brain persons may have a hard time. They are stuck with the ideas and concepts they already know and cannot make the leap into the new and unknown. They would rather produce a step-by-step recipe than explore unknown territory. They would rather be told what to do or follow directions than have the freedom to create anything they want. They need to learn to develop the right side of the brain's simultaneous thinking to help them with new ideas, make new connections, and imagine new possibilities. They must adapt the right-brain task to the left side of the brain and use their own step-by-step approach to come up with new ideas, or develop the right side of their brain.

There are many tasks that require the right side of the brain. People with mixed preferences may be using the left side for tasks that would be better serviced by the right side of the brain. They, too, need to know which side is appropriate for which task so they can use that side appropriately. Left-brain adaptations are given in Part 4 of this book, which focuses on techniques for learning by using your best learning link.

Mistaken Identity

Many people grow up thinking they have a learning problem or a learning disability when in fact they are just using the wrong techniques to learn. Even today there are thousands of students who are classified as learning disabled when, in fact, a task is not presented in a way that is compatible with their brain hemispheric preference or they have not been taught how to use the side of the brain that matches the task. A learning disability is a "dysfunction of the central nervous system," which means there is an impairment in the circuitry between the senses, the nervous system, and the brain. This impairment can be thought of as a short-circuit in the nervous system that scrambles a message as it travels from the senses to the brain and back to the senses. This situation does not apply to someone with a mixed preference who has no central nervous system dysfunction, but who has just not been taught how to use the right side of the brain for right-brain tasks and the left side for left-brain tasks. Someone with a mixed preference may make the same mistake as someone with a learning disability, but there is a world of difference. The learning disabled person has irreparable damage to the central nervous system. Thus, no matter how many times they do the same task they will not get it. They have to learn how to accomplish the task using different sensory modalities or techniques. But someone with mixed preferences can learn how to use the other side of their brain, or can convert the task to match the side of the brain for which they show a preference. It is not a question of damage, but of usage. They have been using one side of the brain since childhood and it has developed more neural connections, making that side more efficient and rapid. The other side of their brain can be developed also, or the task can be restructured to match the preferred side.

There are many people with mixed preferences who use each side of the brain inappropriately and grew up thinking there was something wrong with them. This may have affected their self-esteem and their motivation to succeed, and they may have actually dropped out of school or not continued on to higher education thinking there was something wrong with them. Only as an adult do many people with mixed preferences discover that they are not "dumb" or "stupid," but that the system they used failed them. They discover that when the instruction matches their learning style they are excellent learners. It is only the approach used during their school career that was wrong, and with a new approach they can finally feel success. In Part 4 you will learn how to convert the language of each side of the brain into the other as a way to make learning easier.

Part 3

Your Superlink to Accelerated Learning

8

The Eight Superlinks to Accelerated Learning: Which One Is Yours?

Our best learning link is a combination of our learning style and our brain hemispheric preference. In the previous chapters you read about your best learning style and your brain hemispheric preference. That data will now be combined into one profile that makes up your superlink: learning style plus brain hemispheric preference. In chapters 10 to 17 you will find out how you learn according to your superlink: visual left-brain, visual right-brain, auditory left-brain, auditory right-brain, tactile left-brain, tactile right-brain, kinesthetic left-brain, or kinesthetic right-brain.

When we talk about these eight categories, we also need to realize that each person is unique. No two learners are exactly alike. Even two visual right-brain learners will be different because there are many other factors that affect learning style, such as educational background, upbringing, your personality type as defined by Jungian typology or a Myers-Briggs Type Indicator, or how you use your multiple intelligences. When we are trying to accelerate learning we want to focus on those factors that have a direct bearing on the task and provide a system that is manageable and easy for people to use. I have found that people can understand the four learning styles and the two brain hemispheric preferences, and can multiply the two to make eight categories of superlinks. Beyond that, it becomes too complicated for many people to use. Thus, readers should be aware that there are many more combinations to enter into the formula of who we are. For example, we can always take the sixteen personality types from the Myers-Briggs Type Indicator and factor that into these eight superlinks to have one hundred twenty-eight types. For the sake of simplicity and practicality in this book, I have concentrated only on the eight superlinks. I have found that with most people, the eight learning links alone accelerate learning.

Some people are a mixture of several of these eight categories. For those who have either integrated brain hemispheric preference or a mixed preference, you will have to read the descriptions of both the right-brain and left-brain learners. Some people are visual right-brain and visual left-brain, and auditory right-brain and auditory left-brain learners. Some people use three sensory modalities and the right and left sides of the brain. Some people have developed their whole brain and use all four learning styles with both brain preferences. As you read each category that applies to you, identify with a highlighter, or by making a list or a mind map, which parts of each category are more like you.

There is a difference between how people with different superlinks learn, and learning can be accelerated when it is presented in a way that is compatible with our superlink.

9

Create Your Personal Superlink Profile

As you read about the ewight superlinks in chapters 10 to 17, you will learn about your own superlink and form a profile of how you learn. You should jot down information as you read about your superlink or combination of learning links in the next eight chapters. As you advance further in the book you will use this data, applying this knowledge to learning a subject quickly.

You may find that the chapter on your own superlink describes you completely. If you are a combination of two or more learning links you may also discover that there are portions of several chapters that accurately describe you. This means that your personal profile will contain learning strategies suited for you from a combination of learning links. For example, you may have found that you are a combination of two superlinks: tactile left-brain and visual left-brain. Thus, your personal profile will contain portions of those two chapters.

Since we use each of our senses and both sides of our brain to varying degrees, many combinations of superlinks are possible. Do not feel you have to fit precisely into one category. You may learn through a combination of several learning links. Some people may be fortunate enough to have developed their whole brain and find that all eight learning links fit them!

The descriptions of each superlink given in the next eight chapters are not meant to restrict options for people or form stereotypes. Anyone with any learning style can function well at any task and in any job either by adapting to the situation, approaching the job in a different way, or bringing their own unique perspective to it.

If you find you use a combination of superlinks, pick out the portions from each learning link chapter that apply to you and take notes on these portions. The essential point is that you know what *your* particular combination means for your learning, and know how you can use it to accelerate learning. In this way you will have, in hand, your own personal profile to refer to as you move through Part 4 of this book.

My Superlink Is (or Combination of Superlinks Are):

_____

_____

DIRECTIONS: Read through the chapters on each superlink that fits you and record on your paper the portions of each that describe how you need to learn.

10

Visual Left-Brain Learners

Visual left-brain learners take in visual information and convert it into symbols or language, such as letters, numbers, words, or ideas. Although they are sensitive to their visual environment, they pay particular attention to printed matter—letters, words, or numbers. They label this sensory information with names and words. They think in a step-by-step way, attending to one detail at a time, and file data in a systematic way, either alphabetically, numerically, or chronologically.

Since they like to stay organized, they are often engaged in organizing materials involving words and numbers. They may spend time filing their papers, organizing phone numbers and addresses, keeping their finances up to date, paying bills, doing budgets, scheduling appointments in their offices or homes, keeping up with correspondence, programming their computers, doing spreadsheets, or making sure birthday and anniversary cards are mailed out on time. They may find organized and efficient ways for setting up accounting, payroll, record-keeping, or bookkeeping systems.

To keep their affairs in order they may make charts and graphs. They are good at keeping company records, archiving, setting appointments, making chronologies and timelines, keeping timetables, scheduling, and other such tasks. They do not miss a detail and seldom miss an appointment, as long as it is written down so they can see it.

When they are traveling, they plan everything they are going to see in detail in advance. They collect travel brochures, schedules, and information and make reservations far in advance. They like to stick to their planned schedules and feel uncomfortable when anything interferes with the trips they have already visualized and planned in their minds.

When visual left-brain people think, their eyes tend to look upward towards the ceiling, either upper left or upper right, because they process their thoughts by seeing words or images. Everyone's eyes do this when we picture something mentally, except that visual left-brain people are in that mode more often. Visual left-brain people maintain eye contact with a speaker to help them "listen" better. They will turn in their chairs to follow a speaker around the room with their eyes. Visual left-brain people also need those who are listening to them to give them eye contact as well. They become disturbed when they talk to someone who looks down and away, and will sometimes even say, "Look at me when I am talking to you." They need to understand that the eyes of people having other learning styles move in different directions. Eye movements correspond to the modality in which our brain is processing. Although people who have other learning styles do not maintain steady eye contact with a speaker, it does not mean they are not listening; rather, they listen *better* when their eyes are not continually on the speaker.

Accelerated Learning

Visual left-brain people accelerate their learning by reading and seeing visual materials in the form of language: letters, words, and numbers. They also need eye contact with a speaker. They learn any subject more quickly through reading books and study guides if the information is organized and clearly written in step-by-step order. To learn a language they need to see a vocabulary word, its definition, and visual clues for its pronunciation. To learn math they need to read step-by-step instructions showing them how to do a problem. They tend to be accurate with mathematical calculations. Self-study programs that require reading are excellent for them.

They learn through print materials such as books, magazines, journals, newspapers, technical manuals, guidebooks, instruction books, computers, film strips and overheads with words to be read, videos with captions, faxes, tables, graphs, charts, and posters. Written communication is the best way to get a message across to them. They are quicker at responding to faxes, E-mail, written directions, memos, or letters than to phone calls or verbal communications. Computer programs and electronic communication networks that require reading texts with step-by-step detailed instructions are ideal for visual left-brain people.

Visual left-brain people can study with or without music. Music, noise, or talking does not bother them because they are visually attuned and are not paying attention to the auditory stimuli around them.

Due to their keen sensitivity to visual stimuli they are bothered by visual clutter or disorganization in print material. They recall what they have seen and can spot whether print looks right to them: It is as if they have an automatic spell-checker in their brains. They make excellent proofreaders and copyeditors. They can also spot errors in numerical information such as financial reports, budgets, paychecks, tax returns, restaurant checks, or spreadsheets. These are the people who will take a red pen to circle other people's errors. (It must have been a visual left-brain person who invented proofreader's markings!)

They can learn and remember the rules of writing, grammar, punctuation, and spelling if the material is presented in order with rules and formulas printed out, and they can visually recall the examples they see in a textbook. They need everything in their visual environment to look right, especially printed material.

How-to and step-by-step books and guides written in a clear, sequential manner accelerate the visual left-brain person's learning. They can learn how to build a motor, cook a meal, build an addition to a home, or run a business by reading about it rather than merely observing it.

When working on projects or solving problems, visual left-brain people should outline or sequentially list the steps they need to do to reach solutions so they can see their plan on paper, and make sure they have everything they need to carry out each part of the task. Visual left-brain people make excellent administrators and managers because they are extremely organized and can see a task through to completion.

Visual left-brain people like to learn according to a schedule and deadlines. Keeping an organizer, calendar, or day-timer is ideal for them so they can see their schedule.

To accelerate reading, visual left-brain people must visualize the words and details they read. Since reading words is a visual, sequential, and symbolic activity, they already find reading easy. As they read, they visually record every word in order and can recall the material when questioned. Thus, they tend to do well on tests on memorization of reading material. These people are good test-takers if they have study guides, notes, or textbooks from which to study. Some of them are like walking encyclopedias. Ask them to find a fact and they will not only recall what book they read it in, but where in the book they saw it and what visual material surrounded what they read. They are good at skimming to find needed data.

In the workforce, dealing with print material, either in words or in numbers, is ideal for them. In the world of words they can be found in: administration, management, office work such as preparing reports, filing, secretarial work, scheduling, appointment setting, areas dealing with time-management and efficiency, publishing, writing, editing, word processing, desktop publishing, proofreading, teaching, research in any field, library work, writing copy for advertising, marketing, sales, and writing technical and instructional manuals, reviews and literary criticism. In the world of numbers they can be found in accounting, business, finance, stock brokerage, tax specialization, banking, budgeting, economics, financial planning, insurance, payroll, mathematics, statistics, evaluation and measurement, market research, and computer programming.

Adapting Instruction to a Visual Left-Brain Style

Because visual left-brain people focus well on details, their learning is slowed down when they have to condense or summarize the gist of what they read to get the main idea. Thus, they do better on recall of facts they read, than on getting the big picture or making inferences, since these are unstated and they have not *seen* them written in the text.

They should ask instructors for visual material such as outlines, study guides, or notes in sequential order on a board or paper to help them see what is important. In this way they can see it, read along, or ask questions to organize the information in their mind. They can make their own notes by writing themselves or taking dictation in a sequential organized way, such as outlining or making a graphic organizer, so they can see the material in their mind. They may need to find their own sequentially written books and materials that correspond with the subject in order to learn it on their own.

11

Visual Right-Brain Learners

Visual right-brain learners take in information through their eyes and are attuned to images, pictures, graphics, colors, shapes, designs, sizes, and spatial relations. They process and think about this stimuli in a simultaneous way, seeing the whole picture at once. Only after they grasp the big picture can they focus on its details.

They are attuned to the way things look and are bothered by visual clutter. They notice when the colors in a room do not match or if an object is out of place. They make good interior decorators, and with their keen sense of visual balance and design they have a good eye for what accessories go together in a room and can rearrange one until it looks visually pleasing. This same sensitivity makes them notice how people look and dress. They like clothes that look good and use their great eye for color and design to select matching clothes and accessories. They enjoy having their own clothes, skin, hair, or face look good as well as making others look good. Some may tell others when their hair is out of place, their tie does not match their suit, or a button is open. They are so keenly aware of how things look they can become distracted unless the disturbing visual appearance is fixed.

They like to produce work that looks visually appealing in design and color. These are the people to whom others come for attractive presentation packets, color photocopies, attractively bound reports, and visual aids. Visual right-brain learners are the ones who beautify the world. They will hang paintings in a room, keep attractive posters around the office, and bring in flower arrangements. People call on them to decorate the office for the staff party.

They may like going to art galleries, photo exhibits, fashion shows, auto shows, or sightseeing. They may get pleasure from looking at beautiful homes, gardens, cars, boats, horse or animal shows—anything that can be seen. They may enjoy the visuals of the theater, a circus, a museum, a zoo, a park, gardens, or amusement parks with fascinating sights to see.

While they do not keep their things in an organized, linear way like their left-brain counterparts do, they want their visual surroundings to be appealing and will find a way to keep their things in an attractive way. Although they may not be filers, they will have attractive organizers such as colorful boxes, stylish containers, decorative pencil holders, and storage units for their belongings.

Since visual right-brain people think and remember mostly in images, their eyes tend to look upward toward the ceiling, either upper left or upper right. When they are listening they maintain good eye contact and are often watching the movements of the speaker's mouth as well as facial expressions. Visual right-brain people also need their listeners to look at them when they talk and will even request others to do so.

Visual right-brain people go with the flow and end up being *in* the flow, often becoming so absorbed in their projects that they lose track of time. Since time awareness is not in the right side of the brain, they start and finish work on their own time according to the demands of the project rather than the clock.

Accelerated Learning

The best way for visual right-brain people to learn is through visual aids with graphic and pictorial content that allow them to see the big picture. They do not learn from or remember texts or numbers as well unless they are presented using color, shape, design, special calligraphy, or an artistic font.

Many visual right-brainers do not respond to verbal instructions and will do nothing until given visual directions on paper with pictorial images, diagrams, or charts. Pure lecture does not work because they have to work hard at concentrating on auditory stimuli. When they can see a speaker, graphics, and visual aids, their best learning modality is open and whatever talking comes in, coupled with the visual stimuli, will be received and recalled. They learn and remember better by having eye contact with a speaker rather than listening to an audiotaped lecture, but the speaker must also give them something to look at in pictorial form.

If they do not have anything to look at, they should listen to the descriptive words in a lecture so they can paint a mental picture for themselves. They will have a hard time understanding what others are saying unless they are provided with descriptions of color, size, or shape to visualize.

They need to see books, magazines, and overheads with illustrations, pictures, drawings, paintings, or photographs and slides, videos, and movies with people and beautiful, visual, and scenic imagery so they can see what you are talking about. Seeing live examples, real-life objects, demonstrations, enactments, videos, movies, television, slides, or photographs are other stimuli that help them understand and learn. They like computer programs with good graphics and visual images that operate using icons and pictorial directions, rather than detailed, sequential directions.

Visual right-brain people can work with or without music. Music, noise, and talking do not distract them because they are more focused on what they are seeing than what they are hearing.

When describing events or experiences from the past, visual right-brain people will recall images they saw in real life, movies, photographs, and videos, the surroundings, and what people looked like. They are great at spotting famous personalities and people they know in different contexts by matching visual features.

It is easier for them to do math problems when there is a photograph or a pictorial image to accompany the problem as an example. If they are multiplying 24 by 3, they want to see a picture of twenty-four people each holding three slices of pizza.

Using intuition, experimentation, and discovery, they can uncover new ways to do things and find solutions to problems. They make associations easily and one image will bring others to mind. This makes them good at learning through brainstorming or making connections. Since they think things through in a simultaneous way, before starting a project, they first need to know the end product, goal, or bottom line. Once they see the big picture the connections between every part make sense to them. After they get the big picture they are impatient with step-by-step directions and want to jump in and figure it out for themselves as they do it.

Visual right-brain people can accelerate their reading by converting a text into images so they can see what they are reading in their head. This dramatically improves their comprehension. It is hard for the visual right-brain person to grasp words that do not invoke images, such as articles like *a* and *the,* verb tenses, or prepositions. Many tend to focus on words that can be pictured and skip over these small abstract words that cannot be pictured, like *the*, *that*, or *and*, or they substitute *the* for *a*, and vice versa. Thus, on a test, they score higher on questions that contain visual imagery and lower on those that cannot be visualized. If they need to pass an examination or master abstract material, they need to develop the right-brain technique for visualizing everything, even abstract words.

In the workforce, you will find visual right-brain people engaged in the fine arts and graphic design. With their expert eye they may be artists, illustrators, painters, sculptors, jewelry makers, clothing designers, fashion illustrators, interior decorators, beauticians, cosmetologists, or hairdressers. They may be involved in graphic arts, commercial illustration, advertising, or designing posters, brochures, sales pieces, or billboards. In the publishing world they may be art directors, children's book illustrators, the layout and design people, and those that make "beautiful" books. They make good photographers, and you will find their work beautifying magazines, books, brochures, booklets, and other print media.

Other activities they may enjoy are floral arranging, landscaping, or architecture. They want their visual surroundings to be beautiful. They may be the ones to design stationery, greeting cards, or new forms of calligraphy or typography fonts.

As engineers they want to design buildings, structures, or transportation vehicles that look good. They make good car designers, coming up with new sleek, beautiful models.

Adapting Instruction to a Visual Right-Brain Style

Visual right-brain learners need to ask instructors to provide visual images showing the global overview. They need to see the big picture using pictorial images, mind maps, real-life objects or demonstrations, or find their own materials. Since auditory presentations are difficult, they need to see a written copy of a lecture or write their own so they can read at their own pace, converting each word into: a mental image; a colorful illustration; a mind map of the main topic, the details, and their interconnections; or words and numbers written in colorful, decorative calligraphy or design so they can "see" the material.

12

Auditory Left-Brain Learners

The best way for auditory left-brain learners to learn is by hearing the new material presented in the form of language, either words or numbers, in a detailed, step-by-step way. They also think by speaking their thoughts aloud and conversing aloud with others. They work well with accurate data, facts, figures, and statistics and make excellent researchers, often backing up their lectures and presentations with information that supports their topic and gets their ideas across.

They are sensitive to the quality of other people's speech, noticing mistakes in dialogue, such as grammatical and syntactical errors, poor usage of words, repetitive phrases, and poor delivery. They become uncomfortable when speakers drone on or use repetitive language, inappropriate pauses, or too many "ums." Being conscious of speech, they are careful to be good speakers themselves and make great orators. They plan out and rehearse what they are going to say, making sure their sentences are grammatically correct and their language is precise and clear, with appropriate word choices. Many are conscious of timing and phrasing, pausing at the right place for added effect and modulating their voices in a way to keep their audiences engaged. They also make good editors, not for finding visual errors in spelling, but for being conscious of how the text should sound when read aloud. They enjoy collecting words and relish putting them together in interesting ways. They like fancy words, such as *cogitate* for *think*, and words that sound good and provide the closest shade of meaning.

They are great conversationalists, and enjoy talking to a wide range of people. Their great auditory recall manifests itself in their speech when they quote other people like an automatic verbal playback system, replaying conversations almost word-for-word. They can be the life of the party with their storehouse of humorous anecdotes, interesting tidbits from current events and history, the wit and wisdom they heard from others, and their excellent verbal presentation skills. They can relate famous quotations, jokes, riddles, tales, poetry, and lines from the classics, movies, or lectures almost verbatim.

They need constant auditory stimuli. They cannot handle absolute silence. If it is too quiet they feel uncomfortable, and will provide the auditory stimuli themselves by humming, singing, whistling, talking aloud, turning on a radio talk show, television, or audiotape lecture, or calling someone on the telephone. In an office or classroom, when it is too quiet, the auditory people will start talking, wanting to discuss everything. They will either ask many questions or talk to people nearby. If no one will respond to them they may just start talking to themselves aloud. The only time they need silence is when they are studying or reading, because music, noise, or the talking of others distracts them from "hearing" their own thoughts.

Even though they do not maintain steady eye contact with a speaker, because when listening, people's eyes tend to move left and right in the direction of their ears, they are good listeners and will ask a speaker many questions. Although their discussions can become lengthy because they speak with so much sequential, analytical detail, their questions make others feel understood and appreciated.

Because auditory left-brain people think by speaking aloud, some have a tendency to repeat what people around them say, either in their own way or a better one. This may be annoying to others, but auditory left-brain people are not doing this to be rude; they only repeat what others say to think about it more clearly. They also seem to make a running commentary on everything that is happening around them and may sound to others as if they are criticizing or analyzing everything. They are not trying to be critical—they just speak all their thoughts aloud when other people would keep their thoughts to themselves. Auditory left-brain people may need to understand this tendency, lest they unintentionally turn other people off.

They work sequentially and will keep their files and papers orderly. Some enjoy the sequential aspect of working with mathematics by doing number and logic puzzles and solving math problems in everyday life. Some understand the highly mathematical and sequential processes involved in economics, stocks, taxes, and finances and enjoy reading financial papers and business journals, keeping up with the stock market and the business world. They like to keep their financial records, both personal and business, straight, and like to be organized at tax time to do their returns.

Left-brain auditory people who are musically inclined enjoy listening to music and going to concerts, theater, or musicals. Reading music is a left-brain task because it involves converting musical sounds into symbols and vice versa. When they listen to music they are conscious of the technical aspects and analyze it according to their own high standards, judging its technical execution such as the arrangement or a singer's voice quality, which makes them excellent music critics.

Accelerated Learning

Auditory left-brain people can accelerate their learning by listening and talking. In the classroom, or in seminars, they learn through lectures, oral presentations, and discussion. They recall details of conversations, lists, chores, words to a song, or anything else if it is told to them in a step-by-step way. When learning how to fix a car, program a computer, or play a sport, they learn better by listening to directions than by watching someone else perform the task. When memorizing material for a test, they need to hear the material, talk about it, reread it aloud, or tape themselves reading aloud and then play it back several times.

They grasp the meaning of verbal communication quickly without having to convert it into pictures. They can closely follow a college lecture, a verbal training session on the job, or auditory directions, while others of different learning styles may be saying, "What did the speaker say? I don't get it." Auditory left-brain people usually find others clustering around them asking them to explain announcements given over a P.A. system or to repeat the new policies that the boss explained at a meeting.

This group can be found attending lectures and seminars, or taking the audiotaped or guided tours through museums. Some are so absorbed in listening to a lecture during a sightseeing trip that they forget to look at the sights!

Auditory media such as CD's, tape recorders, audiobooks, computers, movies, videos, radio, and television are good learning tools for them. They may relax by listening to news or talk shows on the radio while driving, or watching the evening news or a television documentary after work. They also enjoy reading books, news magazines, newspapers, and professional journals because as they read they hear the words in their head. Audio computer programs, verbal presentations, or texts presented in a step-by-step way are the best learning tools for them.

They can learn well from technical manuals and instructional guides if they read them aloud. They are also good at writing them. These are the people who know how to program a computer or a VCR. If you do not already have an auditory left-brain friend you may want to search for one, because these are the people who understand the way things work in this technological age, based on the language of words, numbers, and computer terminology carried out in a logical, step-by-step way.

Many enjoy history, current events, and biographies because these are sequential, chronological, and verbal genres.

They are sensitive to auditory distractions. When they are listening to a speaker, they become annoyed if anything distracts them. A passing car, a humming heater, or someone crunching chips will drive them out of their minds. Since they cannot tune out distractions as visual people can, they carefully orchestrate their listening environment to hear only the speaker or only their own thoughts. They have a hard time concentrating or studying with background music and need quiet to read and study. Headphones may help them concentrate when there is too much auditory distraction.

Many auditories enjoy debate. They work well in teams and cooperative groups that involve discussion, and use this continual feedback to restructure and regroup their own thoughts.

To comprehend better, they need to either read aloud, read softly to themselves, or hear words in their mind. They need to stop frequently and ask themselves questions about what they read. They also need to hear what they read in a step-by-step way to grasp the material. If they read material that jumps from one idea to another without any order, they need to restructure it in their minds by asking questions in order to convert it into a step-by-step process and form an outline or study guide. They do not enjoy books that ramble on going nowhere, but those that are sequentially organized and move to a logical conclusion or resolution.

In the workforce they can be found in jobs that require listening and talking in a step-by-step way. They may be public speakers, sales and marketing people, receptionists, lawyers, politicians, administrators, presenters, lecturers, college professors, teachers, disc jockeys, musicians, singers, songwriters, editors, writers, poets, actors and actresses, announcers, emcees, broadcasters, such as television news anchors, sportscasters, announcers in commercials, or audiobook readers. Some become mathematicians, accountants, bookkeepers, bankers, financial planners, tax specialists, economists, and stockbrokers.

No matter what their careers, auditory left-brain people are the workers asked to do tasks that involve speaking, listening, or giving oral presentations and training to the staff, clients, or trainees, because words and numbers are their medium for communication with the world.

Adapting Learning to an Auditory Left-Brain Style

Auditory left-brain people should ask an instructor to present material in an auditory, sequential way through lectures and discussion. Auditory left-brain people should use books on tape and should take their own notes in a linear manner. They should read the material aloud and into a tape recorder. They need to study with a partner or discussion group.

13

Auditory Right-Brain Learners

Auditory right-brain learners learn best through hearing and are attuned to sounds, music, rhythms, tones of voice, and strong sensory words that give an overview of the big picture. This group is
sensitive to sounds that others miss. Musical harmony is important
to them because they are particularly bothered by any dissonant
sounds. They are attracted to beautiful sounds, sweet melodies, and
pleasing voices and are repelled by annoying and grating sounds
such as sirens, construction drills, or irritating voices.

They enjoy traveling to get away from the dissonant sounds
of a city to spend time relaxing amidst the sounds of nature in
the mountains, a forest, or by the ocean. To keep the sounds at
home or in their office pleasant, many have a good selection of
tapes for background music. Some enjoy environmental sound
tapes such as the sounds of the ocean, rain, birds in the forest,
or running brooks.

They have a good ear for music. They enjoy going to concerts, musicals, jazz brunches, music clubs, or religious and social
ceremonies with musical services or presentations. While not
adept at the language of words, they are like tape recorders when

it comes to music. They can hear a tune, remember it exactly, and sing it or pick up an instrument and play it perfectly by ear. Many auditory right-brain people in the music field may not have had any formal music training and cannot read music; they just make music and it sounds great. They spend time practicing and creating their own songs and instrumentals. They may create a song, tune, or whole symphony in their heads and then reproduce it with instruments or by singing. It is as if they are tapped into an internal CD player that creates new melodies and songs.

Auditory right-brainers get creative ideas for sound effects, often coming up with new types of sounds, new genres of music, new instruments, or new combinations of instruments and sounds, such as the combination of music and the sounds of nature.

Right-brain auditories feel uncomfortable when there is no auditory stimulus. They will create it by turning on music or making auditory stimuli themselves, such as singing, humming, whistling, tapping a beat, making their mouth sound like instruments or sound effects, mimicking voices or people's accents, or doing impersonations or cartoon character's voices.

Although they do not maintain direct eye contact with a speaker, because their eyes move side to side in the direction of their ears, they are acutely aware of nonverbal communication and tones of voice. They can pick up on someone's negativity, hidden anger, resentment, and sarcasm. Conversely, they can also pick up someone's sincerity and loving, caring, and kind attitude and will immediately respond to that person. Others may think they are mind readers because they can grasp people's true meaning from subtle nuances of tone in face-to-face and telephone conversations, no matter what words are used to hide the speaker's feelings. Auditory right-brain people appear to be deep, not saying much, but understanding all.

They enjoy being with people who do not stress their verbal auditory system. Some like to talk a lot to friends about their interests and hobbies, usually getting to the point quickly, and changing topics frequently, while others like to be with people with whom they can relax, not have to talk much, and with whom they can communicate with few words or strong sensory language.

Accelerated Learning

Auditory right-brain people can accelerate their learning by listening to sound, music, and strong sensory language that give an overview or big picture. They learn more from the sounds of words than from a printed text. When they are memorizing material for a test or speech, it is better for them to hear someone else read the material or write down the information themselves and read it aloud, talk about it, or tape-record it so they can play it back several times. They remember words better and can repeat them verbatim if they are combined with music, rhymes, rhythm, catchy songs and tunes, jingles in commercials and advertisements, poetry, raps, beats, environmental sounds, or by mimicking distinctive voice qualities or accents. They recall a story conveyed in a musical, or the words to a song on music videos. As children, they learned the alphabet by singing the alphabet song. Their best learning pathway is open when words and numbers are tied to music.

This group, which is not attuned to symbolic, abstract language, does not learn well from lectures unless the speaker gets to the point and uses sensory words. They need to hear the bottom line and the whole concept. When other people's conversation becomes too abstract, detailed, and sequential, some auditory right-brain people may either cut them off and say, "I get it," because they have grasped the whole idea, or they tune out, drift off, and hum a song, tap a beat, or even sing while the other person is still speaking. They will refocus on the lecture only when the speaker gets to the point.

Live music, CD's and tapes, slide shows with music, movies, videos, television, computers, CD-ROM programs, and video games with good music and sound effects are the best learning materials for them. Imaginative, interactive computer programs that use sound effects, voices, and music are also good.

They understand better when words are tied to movies, videos and real-life demonstrations because of the right brain's excellent visual-spatial memory. They can remember learning material better by mentally converting words into a movie, with sound effects, imagined music, and dialogue being acted out. This association technique helps auditory right-brain people learn abstract subjects such as grammar, spelling, vocabulary, foreign languages, or algebra, traditionally taught in a left-brain way.

To remember procedures, auditory right-brain people need to visualize each action, and discuss it aloud, understanding the global overview first and then filling in the details. Their study partner should go over each step slowly and carefully with them, ask them to repeat the material back, and check their accuracy.

When writing, speaking, or reading they tend to get to the point quickly and often leave out the unimportant, abstract words. They sometimes mix up words or letters. They may come up with a word other than the one they mean; for example, meaning to say "dog" but instead saying "cat" because of their close association. Also, they may read the first few letters of a word and intuitively try to figure out the rest of the word, thus coming out with a word that sounds close to the right one but is not correct. They get a global impression instead of reading each letter, in order.

When doing math, they understand broad concepts or processes but may not attend to the specific details of checking their work, doing step-by-step processes, or proving their answers. They can get an answer intuitively by finding relationships and patterns and grasping the whole process, but when it comes to the details of calculations, they may make errors. They may see a multiple-digit number simultaneously and come up with the first response that comes to mind. Thus, they may read 378 as 738 or 873. Others may think they have dyslexia, but they do not—it is just that their right brain reads everything simultaneously instead of in linear order.

Since language is usually located in the left hemisphere of the brain, auditory people with a right-brain preference may have poor listening skills and may not be able to follow spoken language quickly. They often need directions repeated several times in order to grasp them and will ask those around them, "What did the speaker say? What are the directions?" Since they mostly grasp words that carry sensory stimuli they may miss important abstract words such as *not*, *if*, *after*, *before*, and other prepositional phrases. Thus, if they hear "Do not read this," they may pick up only "Do read this," causing them to make mistakes in school or on the job. Auditory right-brain people need to learn coping strategies. Those who are speaking to them should also understand that auditory right-brain people need instructions to be given slowly, one item at a time, often repeated two or three times, with sensory imagery if possible. They need the extra milliseconds to access each word as an image in the right side of the brain and convert it back into words by processing language in the left side of the brain.

Because they are easily distracted by sounds, they need an environment in which only one auditory stimulus is going on at once, whether it is a speaker or music. Headphones are a good way for them to shut out unwanted sounds when they are learning.

Auditory right-brain learners think mostly intuitively, without words. They pick up meaning from music, sounds in the environment, and people's tones of voice. Left-brain people may marvel at how someone can think and learn without words, but it is a different kind of learning—it is an instantaneous knowledge that does not require words, like two friends knowing what the other is thinking without even talking.

To accelerate reading, right-brain auditory people first need an overview of the reading material. Then, as they read they can fit the details into the whole picture. They need to imagine the text as a movie with sound effects, accents and tones of voice, feelings, and music to make the material come alive. Vocabulary describing sound attracts their attention.

Auditory right-brain learners comprehend better when they read aloud, or if that is disruptive to others they should read softly, or hear the words in their head. Since they are better at grasping an overview of what they are reading, they tend to miss details that may affect the meaning. On comprehension tests they get the gist of what they read, but have difficulty with specific facts about time order, sequence, or questions about details.

To overcome this right-brain tendency, they need auditory right-brain techniques to get them to slow down, pay attention, and read words from left to right, letter by letter, without skipping any words. By using pointers, guides, or highlighters as they read aloud they can monitor their progress. Visualization techniques help them experience what they are reading and can help them improve their retention of smaller details and abstract time words and prepositions. They can talk about what they are experiencing as they do this, as an auditory reinforcement of their visualization.

In the workforce, you may find auditory right-brain people in jobs that require listening to sounds, music, and nature in a global, simultaneous way. They may be musicians, songwriters, members of a rock group, jazz trio or quartet, rhythm and blues group, orchestra, or band. Auditory right-brain people are so sensitive to sound and its variations that they are the ones who make good sound mixers and editors for a recording studio, concert hall, or music, movie, or video production company. Some may become the sound effects or special effects technicians for a movie, CD-ROM software, television, or video production company.

Whatever their profession, auditory right-brain learners are low-key, laid-back people who enjoy harmony—and music, and the positive vibrations that flow from people around them.

Adapting Learning to an Auditory Right-Brain Style

Auditory right-brain people can ask an instructor to enhance their lectures with short sensory language, music, or sound effects, along with images, mind maps, real-life objects, or demonstrations. Because many lectures are too fast-paced for them to follow while taking notes, they need to get a printed study guide, text, or tape recording so they can work at their own pace to convert the words into a mental movie, into drawings of the information with key words highlighted, or idea webs that show the main topic and the details. They need to participate in real-life situations or find materials that give an overview and use sensory words and visual aids that correspond to the subject, and work at their own pace converting it into a movie in their mind while talking about it.

14

Tactile Left-Brain Learners

Tactile left-brain learners learn sequentially through the symbolic language of letters, numbers, and words. They also learn using their hands and fingers, their sense of touch, and their emotions. They often hold a pen or pencil and write to help them think and listen better. If they are told to put their pen away they will find some other object to touch.

They are sensitive to language coupled with nonverbal communication such as a speaker's facial gestures, body language, tone of voice, and mood, which makes them doubly aware of other people's messages. They maintain eye contact mostly to read a speaker's expression and then look down and away when they think. They tend to be able to articulate their own feelings well and can easily empathize with others. They often gesticulate with their hands and are generally expressive. Tactile left-brain people are sensitive to other people's feelings and their own feelings get hurt easily. They think with their hearts and express their thoughts verbally or in writing in terms of feelings. If learning material is tied to a physical or emotional sensation it will be more meaningful to them. They spend time working out relationships, being with family and loved ones, writing letters, or talking on the telephone.

Tactile left-brain people get new ideas as intuition or gut feelings and then conceive of the step-by-step approach for carrying them out. When ideas come, tactile left-brain people feel compelled to write them down sequentially. They may wake up in the middle of the night with an idea and have to write it immediately. They can be passionate about their ideas, and this enthusiasm rubs off on others. They are highly motivated and use their logic and ability to express their feelings in words that convince others of their ideas.

Accelerated Learning

Tactile left-brain people accelerate their learning by participating in activities that require the use of their hands and fingers. They need to write what they see and hear in order to learn in a sequential way. They are interested in words and numbers. In seminars or lectures they may take copious notes in a linear, sequential way, but will never need to look at them again. The act of writing, by itself, helps their brain process information. Many think and listen better when they doodle, draw, or hold something in their hands. Copying material from a text or taking dictation from a lecture enables them to recall the material later. They also recall the order in which they write notes. Because of their left hemispheric dominance they tend to organize notes or make outlines, lists, diagrams, or charts.

For every subject they learn, they require active hands-on experiences with manipulatives to accompany a lecture or seminar. Once they have typed something, they will remember it. They learn by constructing and building things with their hands in a linear, step-by-step way. In science they need to not only perform an experiment (a good hands-on activity), but write about the results. They do not learn well if a teacher just shows and explains new material to them without allowing them to first write it down or guiding them in performing a task so they "get a feel" for doing it.

In order to learn, tactile left-brain people need to use paper, notebooks, blank books, journals, diaries, stationery, pencils, pens, markers, crayons, paints, sculpting materials, arts and crafts, board games, computers, sports equipment that involves the hands, musical instruments, and other hands-on materials. Sequential computer programs that allow them to type, interact on an emotional level, and communicate with others are ideal.

When memorizing material for a test, they will best recall the material they learned by touching, writing, drawing, or experiencing it on an emotional level. They can recall a subject in detail when they can associate the experience with a physical or emotional sensation while learning, and this makes it more meaningful and relevant to them. Visual and auditory details can be remembered if tied to an emotion. Thus, they will remember seeing a smile that conveys warm feelings and remember hearing words conveyed with love. When tactile children learn their language, it is the love of their parents expressed through words that helps the words sink in.

Tactile left-brain people learn well in a peaceful environment, such as a setting in which they can see mountains, trees, or a lake. They need to be comfortable while studying. Many like to stretch out on the floor, recline comfortably on a chair, or lie on a couch. They may be able to type, write, read or study with music, if it is music they like, because they focus on feelings, not words. The good feelings their favorite music brings them help them tune out other negative stimuli, focus on positive feelings, and thus stimulate them to be more productive.

They need positive feelings in order to concentrate or they may shut down. And they cannot concentrate when they feel others do not like them. Negative vibrations from others, both verbal and nonverbal, need to be minimized. If they feel emotionally uncomfortable, tactile left-brain people use language in an organized, clear way to question others about what they are really feeling based on their tones of voice, and will talk with others to straighten out the situation. If they cannot talk about their feelings, they can write them as poetry, essays, or journal entries.

Tactile people can benefit from learning in cooperative teams or groups. They thrive on positive feelings from group members with whom they feel comfortable, and whose appreciative words and warm touches help them work better. If their socializing distracts others, tactile left-brain people can be encouraged instead to write to their friends in class. Socializing with others does not hinder their ability to listen and work, but actually increases their interest in their work.

To accelerate reading, tactile left-brain people need to internalize what is happening. They need to feel what the words describe and what the characters are feeling. They are bored if they cannot emotionally identify with the reading material.

If they are reading about abstract subjects they should try to feel what is happening. For example, if they are reading about a chemical reaction, they need to become one of the chemicals and experience rising up as a gas themselves. If they are reading a biography, they need to feel what the person would have lived through on a physical and emotional level. They can actually recall everything they read if they convert it into a feeling. What they do not convert into a feeling can be lost.

In whatever they read, they will also remember it better if they jot down their ideas as they read. They may read books or novels that have depth, feeling, and a powerful message. They may read self-help and how-to books to solve a problem, to help them deal with feelings and relationships, or to learn something important for their jobs or life skills. They prefer it if these topics were written in a step-by-step, logical way.

In the workforce, you may find them in jobs that require the use of their hands and fingers, or emotions that involve working in a step-by-step way. They tend to be structured and organized in their work. If they go into the fine arts, they approach the work in a detailed way. When they draw they tend to be good at copying what they see in detail and paying more attention to the technical aspects of the art. They may enter the commercial arts and do layout, design, fashion illustration, children's book illustrations, or advertising.

Some play instruments or write music and songs because these activities involve both their hands and fingers and their feelings.

They may be involved in farming, gardening, floral arranging, architecture, drafting, city planning, designing electronic and technological equipment, technical writing, electrical engineering, construction, building, landscaping, painting, plumbing, wallpapering, the restaurant business, or cooking. When sewing, knitting, building models, doing arts and crafts, woodworking, sculpting, basket-weaving, or making textiles, jewelry, pottery, or designing, they learn by reading the instructions and working in a step-by-step way. They may also work in film-making, photography, dance, or theater. Because they are so attuned to feelings they also make good actors and actresses.

As writers, tactile left-brainers produce narratives, essays, journalistic forms of writing like newspaper and magazine articles, advertising copy, biographies, history with a humanistic approach, how-to and self-help books, educational, informational, or technical instructions or manuals to help people do their jobs better. They offer clear, practical, step-by-step solutions. If they write fiction, screenplays, poetry, or children's books, they tend to learn the formulas and rules for writing. They may be involved with desktop publishing programs and do their writing, artwork, and layout on a computer. If they give lectures or training, they first write out a speech in a structured outline, and then follow the outline. They speak with passion and feeling in a clear, logical way.

Many are involved in step-by-step sports that involve their hands, and learn them by writing the instructions for how their body should move or the rules of the game. If someone is explaining a tennis stroke to them, they do better if they can take notes about it, think it through, feel themselves doing it first, perform it, and have a coach give feedback so they can adjust the stroke until they get it right.

Many tactile left-brain people get involved in careers that deal with feelings, help people, or alleviate suffering, such as medicine, science, social work, education, psychology, relationship work, therapy, humanitarian projects, running social organizations or family shelters, ecology projects, helping the homeless, the poor, the needy, or orphans, or working for peace. Whatever their careers, they reach others' hearts by involving their feelings and touching them in a deep way.

Adapting Learning to a Tactile Left-Brain Style

Tactile left-brain people should ask an instructor to let them take notes from a lecture or seminar or from printed outlines, study guides, or data presented in sequential order. For taking sequential notes on their own, they need sequentially organized books and other written or audio-visual materials. They can talk to an instructor or coworkers about their need for positive communication and feedback. If there is no change in a negative environment, they can write their thoughts and feelings in a journal or talk to someone. They can also learn relaxation techniques and coping skills to deal with their sensitive feelings.

15

Tactile Right-Brain Learners

Tactile right-brain learners are sensitive people who tend to think globally. They look at the big picture or overview, and they learn using their hands and fingers, their sense of touch, and their emotions. They use intuition, imagination, language that expresses feelings, and sensory words. They are adept at reading nonverbal communication and also express themselves in a nonverbal way by making faces or sounds of pleasure and displeasure, or by gesticulating. They are sensitive to others' feelings and their own are easily hurt. They are moved by sad or touching parts of movies and books.

Loving relationships are important to them because they need to "feel good" emotionally to function. They spend a great deal of time communicating, either on the phone or face to face so they can read other people's nonverbal expressions and tones of voice. They maintain eye contact mostly to read others' expressions and will look down and away to think.

Tactile right-brain people think with their hearts. They get new ideas and information intuitively. They feel passionately about these ideas and can be very persuasive when relaying their ideas to others. They may not be detailed or systematic in bringing the idea into reality but often jump in and do it impulsively. They have the end product in mind and will try to get there as quickly as possible without worrying about details.

Since they do not need to think in terms of words, but only ideas, they can understand new information quickly because they can comprehend the whole picture instantaneously. They often startle those around them by accurately guessing what the other person is thinking. They can get the gist of a two-hour lecture in moments through intuition.

They work in an original and imaginative way. They often come up with new images and designs that no one has thought of before. As writers, they gravitate to imaginative kinds of writing. In the arts, they create new art forms or new ways of presenting old forms. They use art to express their feelings. They may be involved with arts and crafts, sewing, knitting, textiles, pottery, basket-weaving, jewelry-making, or woodworking. Some like to play an instrument and create their own original and imaginative music and songs. They can play by ear and pick out a tune without reading music.

Some tactile right-brain people enjoy games and sports that involve their hands. Since they do not have the patience for the constraint of organized games with long directions, rules, and regulations, they prefer to play for fun. They do not necessarily play to win, but for the social contact with people they like, or because they like the feel of the game. When learning these games they tend to just jump in and perform, getting a feel for them as they go along and learning by trial and error. Many prefer free-form games and sports in which they can be creative in their moves, such as dance, gymnastics, ice skating, roller skating or Rollerblading, or swimming.

Accelerated Learning

Tactile right-brain people can accelerate their learning by involving their hands, fingers and feelings. Since they are not attuned to symbolic language, they learn through sensory language or nonverbal communication that gives the big picture. They learn by sketching and drawing pictures, diagrams, illustrations, maps, and making sculptures, models, or artistic booklets of what they hear and learn.

They may take notes by drawing but never need to look at them again. They remember new material better when they take notes using calligraphy or colorful, artistically-drawn letters. The act of drawing or writing artistically helps them understand and remember the material. When listening to seminars, talking on the phone, or speaking to someone they may doodle or jot down quick sketchy notes, pictorial icons, diagrams, or mind maps in a way that shows the relationships between the points. Since they are not auditorially attuned to abstract language, it helps if they can see visuals or graphics they can copy.

To listen or think better, they need to do or hold something with their hands. It could be a pen, paintbrush, clay, a computer mouse, or any object. If they are told not to touch anything they will fidget, play with objects, tap their fingers on their desk, or play with their hair.

They also need the big picture, not the small details, or they will be lost. They may become impatient with lengthy written directions, and would rather just try to get a feel for the project at hand. When learning how to do a math problem they need to see the whole problem with the answer and all the steps mapped out. They should then try to do it themselves. The right side of the brain is adept at figuring out mathematical patterns just from seeing the problem and its solution and similar examples several times. When memorizing material for a test, they recall what they felt, touched, drew, or wrote. The subject needs to be tied to their physical or emotional responses.

Tactile right-brain people need hands-on experiences and manipulatives to learn. Lecturing or reading directions will not be as effective unless their hands can be involved. Writing and illustrating the table of elements help them remember it. Hitting the key strokes helps them learn a software program.

If it is not possible to use their hands, they need to use their imagination to visualize themselves doing a task with their hands and feeling the sensation in their mind. Tactile right-brain people need the following learning materials: sketch pads, drawing paper, notebooks, blank books, diaries, pencils, pens, markers, crayons, paints, sculpting materials, and arts and crafts materials. In math, using objects, calculators, or manipulatives helps them learn faster. Real-life items, such as tools and equipment from all fields, board games, sports equipment, or musical instruments can help them learn many subjects. They like the more free-flowing, nonsequential aspect of the computer offered by the use of the mouse, or user-friendly programs that require a click on an icon. Their tactile dexterity can also make them quick at typing. They may also learn about graphics to create computer art or layouts in desktop publishing programs.

They learn best in a positive learning environment that is physically and emotionally comfortable. Negative nonverbal communications from others need to be eliminated. Due to their sensitivity to nonverbal communication their right brain picks up sarcastic tones, resentment, hatred, annoyance, and other negative feelings. When they hear these tones, their openness to learning shuts down. They may withdraw or respond nonverbally, expressing resentment through defiant looks, resistant body language, and negative tones of voice. Their attentiveness increases when they are not distracted by the negative feelings of others.

Coaches or instructors can help them refine their technique if they offer help in a positive way when asked, but they need to be careful that the tactile right-brain person does not perceive any negative tones or they will turn off to them. It is better to wait until the tactile right-brain person asks for advice first before offering it, lest it be taken the wrong way.

Tactile right-brain people like to work in a peaceful environment or a natural setting. They need to be comfortable while studying, and will stretch out on the floor or in a chair, or lie on the couch. They can learn with or without music, but it has to be music they like or they will be disturbed. They are not distracted by music when they read or study because they do not focus on words; they get a wholistic impression of the music, its message and mood from the tune and the words, and pick up positive feelings. Some enjoy music that combines the sounds of nature with pleasant music. Music has a calming, relaxing influence, minimizes sad and negative feelings, lifts their spirits, and increases their ability to learn.

Working in cooperative teams or with one or two people they enjoy can increase their ability to learn because they thrive on the positive feelings from others. Praise, appreciation, and positive nonverbal expression accelerate their learning.

To accelerate reading, tactile right-brain people need to feel the written message or identify on an emotional level with the subject or character. They can thumb through a book, open a page, and find whatever information they need without reading all of it. They will often skip over details and lengthy explanations to get to the bottom line.

They like books that touch their emotions and become bored if they cannot relate to the emotional interaction between characters. When reading about abstract subjects they may personify the material to make it come alive.

Books that are rich in imagination and have depth, feeling, or a powerful message appeal to them. They like how-to and self-help books dealing with feelings and relationships. After reading, they remember the text if they make sketches, drawings, or iconic symbols as they go along. They take notes by writing key words, preferably in color or with an artistic design. Writing their notes in a pictorial or diagram form, such as a mind map, helps them remember them better.

In the workforce they may be writers, artists, photographers, film-makers, or musicians. They may work in engineering, architecture, city planning, technical writing, designing electronic and technical equipment, drafting, electrical work, construction, building, farming, gardening, landscaping, floral arrangement, painting, plumbing, wallpapering, cooking, the restaurant business, or any field involving their hands. They can find easier, more efficient, and more creative ways of doing these jobs and will look at them through paradigms that no one had thought of before.

Some may be involved with film-making, photography, dancing, or acting, often looking at life in new ways. If they go into acting they are good at portraying the feelings of other people. Their sensitivity to other people's feelings may involve them in professions that allow them to alleviate others' suffering or help people, such as social work, psychology, therapy, education, medicine, health, humanitarian projects, or peace movements.

Adapting Learning to a Tactile Left-Brain Style

Tactile left-brain people should ask an instructor to provide the big picture using short, sensory language. They should be allowed to draw, do hands-on projects, or make a mind map in a global, creative, free-flowing way. Since it is hard for them to follow auditory presentations, they need a written copy of notes or readings complete with illustrations. They should convert each word at their own pace into a mental movie, colorful, artistic, and creative drawings, mind maps showing the main topic and details and their interconnections, hands-on projects, or decorative and colorfully written words, calligraphy, or designs. They need to observe real-life demonstrations and draw a mind map that gives the big picture.

16

Kinesthetic Left-Brain Learners

Kinesthetic left-brain learners think in an organized, systematic way and learn through moving their large motor muscles. Because the language function is in the left side of the brain, they can verbalize movement activities in systematic, structured ways.

They need to move a great deal and are restless when they have to stay in one place. If they are forced to stay in one seat too long they will begin to move or rock in the seat, kick their legs, or get out of the seat spontaneously. Others may be distracted by their movements. But if they are given an opportunity to use their body they will actually stick to a task with great concentration; it is when they are denied movement that they find some other outlet for their kinesthetic needs that may not be productive. They are going to move anyway, whether restricted or not—so at least the lessons should be structured in a way that includes movement as a positive part of their training.

They like team sports, organized games, or exercises that have rules and are done in a step-by-step way. Many kinesthetic left-brain people are very coordinated and can time their movements to be in synch with others. They often excel in synchronized swimming, gymnastics, acrobatics, or choreographed dance.

Not all kinesthetic left-brain people are athletic and coordinated, but they still require sequential movement activities in other fields, whether they are developing real estate, designing a CD-ROM program, curing a disease, or exploring a new hobby. Movement for them can be just mentally moving from one topic or project to another. They are systematic and orderly and tend to stick to and complete a task before moving on.

They need room to move around and comfortable sitting areas to stretch out and relax. If a place does not allow them to move about or has no action-oriented activity, kinesthetic left-brain people will feel uncomfortable and bored because there is nothing for them to do there.

They enjoy talking with other people while they are jogging, exercising, or working with someone else.

Accelerated Learning

Kinesthetic left-brain people can accelerate their learning using an organized, systematic, step-by-step approach that involves moving their bodies and muscles. They are language-oriented, so they can describe what they are doing and follow verbal systematic directions for movement activities. They should get on an exercise bike and read or study while pedaling, or walk around the room while memorizing the lines to a play. Learning games, simulations, role-play, and competitions are great ways for them to learn. Whatever movement they do, they prefer to use a formula, structure, or outline for their work.

It may appear to others that kinesthetic people are not listening because they are constantly moving, and they process thought better when their eyes look down and away from a speaker, but they are most attentive when they are in motion. It is so stressful for them to sit still with their eyes on a speaker that they cannot concentrate on listening. Yet when they are moving about they are relaxed, comfortable, and attentive.

Hands-on materials and manipulatives are important to kinesthetics, but they benefit more from moving their entire bodies, not just their hands. The simple act of standing up helps them learn because it gets their leg, arm, and other muscles moving. They need to write with large markers or chalk on a flip chart or chalkboard while standing. Doing math problems or outlining a report on a flip chart helps them to think better. By writing in large letters on a chalkboard, they can involve their arm muscles and take the activity into the kinesthetic realm. Kinesthetic left-brain people doodle or draw because it may be the only movement they are permitted in a constrained work or learning situation. It offers them some movement of their arms and hands, which may not fully satisfy them, but it is better than sitting still.

In whatever subject they learn, they need to learn by doing something in a sequential way. Just listening to lectures and verbal explanations is not enough for them to assimilate the material. They should volunteer to be a demonstrator instead of just watching the demonstration. If they hear action words in sequential order, they will physically understand the material. They need a coach who will actively work through the steps of a process. If they are learning about computer software, they have to be at a computer while going through each step. If they are learning about carpentry, they will need the tools and materials to build something for themselves. They will remember not what an instructor does, but what *they* do.

When memorizing material for a test or examination, they recall what they did with the material. When they study, they need to act out or dramatize the material, either physically or mentally, so they can remember it. If the subject is math or science, they need to work out the problems or experiments in a step-by-step way in real-life applications, for example, by doing the math required for sending a spaceship to the moon, mixing chemicals to produce medicine, or writing a CD-ROM program. If circumstances do not allow a kinesthetic left-brain person to do an activity, their next best resort is to watch activity—movies, television, or videos.

Another kinesthetic method for them is to visualize themselves moving. In this way they can experience action without distracting others.

Kinesthetic left-brain people thrive on achievement, winning, challenges, and discovery. Being goal-oriented, they enjoy the thrill of the game, and their motivation increases in a competitive environment. They like competing with themselves or against teams. Since the left side of the brain handles facts and figures, kinesthetic left-brainers tend to discuss game scores or keep records of achievement of others or themselves.

Kinesthetic left-brain people need manipulatives, organized games, building materials, sports equipment, science projects, large markers, and large pieces of paper, flip charts, erasable boards, computers, musical instruments, hands-on models, kits, or real objects to move. They like structured high-action computer programs, especially CD-ROM. Moving a joystick or a mouse interests them more than just typing on a keyboard.

Kinesthetic left-brain people can read, work, or study with or without music. Moving or dancing to the rhythm and beat of music can stimulate them to work better. When their muscles are in motion stress is reduced, their attention and motivation increase, and they learn faster. Kinesthetic left-brain people enjoy playing musical instruments that engage the whole body. They can handle a systematic approach to learning an instrument and will attend to the technical aspects of playing, such as timing, rhythm, and reading music.

Working in cooperative groups or teams helps kinesthetic left-brain learners because they can move around from group to group. But they like to work from a plan or structured outline so they know each step of the process beforehand. Interaction with different people in different groups fulfills their need to be where the action is.

To accelerate reading, kinesthetic left-brain people should get actively involved in the reading material, either by physically acting out the text or imagining themselves doing so. To engage their interest and remember what they read, they need to mentally convert the words into an action movie. They will forget whatever they do not imagine themselves doing as they read.

Kinesthetic left-brain people prefer to read action-packed books. They like to read about movement-oriented activities in a detailed, step-by-step, well-organized way if it can help them improve what they do. The left brain's ability to think in terms of language helps them understand verbal or written directions for action-oriented subjects. They enjoy how-to books that help them perform better if they are written in logical, sequential ways. Business people enjoy reading how-to suggestions for improving their businesses. Sports lovers enjoy books that help them perfect their techniques.

They need a purpose and an action-oriented reason to be motivated to read. If they know their sales will increase if they read the training manual, they will be sure to read it. If they know they need to pass a driver's license examination, they will force themselves to read the manual.

In the workforce, kinesthetic left-brain people can be found in jobs that require movement along with left-brain organization, putting what they do into words, or giving detailed verbal directions to others. Jobs that require traveling, speaking, and being clear and organized in one's presentation are found in sales, marketing, district management, owning a self-employed business, teaching, and training. Kinesthetic left-brain people who go into the sciences may be involved in experiments, research and laboratory work, or medical fields, becoming doctors and nurses.

Since they excel at movement jobs that are related to being on time, a function of the left side of the brain, they may be pilots, train conductors, chauffeurs, truck drivers, delivery people, or postal workers. Work that involves the physical body and using details, measurements, and precision are construction, farming, engineering, roadwork, painting, wallpapering, plumbing, electrical work, cleaning, furniture crafting, and doing repair work. Jobs that require physically protecting other people and that use the left-brain attention to structure, organization, and rules are in areas such as the armed forces, the police force, fire department, or secret service.

Kinesthetic left-brainers may be involved in organized sports and games or may use their verbal abilities to become sportscasters or coaches and instructors in movement fields such as aerobics, exercise, or dance. They may write action stories, sports columns, reviews of movies, dance, or theatrical performances, or organized and structured how-to books. Their ability to visualize action on a screen or stage may make them good screenwriters and playwrights. As artists they are structured and systematic in their work and will portray detailed action in illustrations, cartoons, comic strips, or advertising. They may be directors of movies, plays, or dance groups. They may become actors and actresses, musicians, performers, or instructors of performing arts that require body movement.

Adapting Learning to a Kinesthetic Left-Brain Style

Kinesthetic left-brain people should ask an instructor to let them do movement activities in a sequential way to learn the material. If instruction is presented as a lecture they need to ask for outlines or study guides, or make their own notes in sequential order on a board or paper so they can convert the words into action, a mental movie in which they have a part, or an outline written in large lettering. They can find sequential materials, either written or in an audio-visual format, that relate to the subject and help them convert the text into action.

17

Kinesthetic Right-Brain Learners

Kinesthetic right-brain learners learn by moving their gross motor muscles in a creative, imaginative, free-flowing, and unstructured way. They do not think in terms of words, but get information intuitively.

They become highly restless if forced to stay still or remain in one place too long. They will feel so constrained and physically stressed that they will start to move around anyway. Their need to keep moving and changing activities may make them look hyperactive to others. It is actually when they are denied movement that they look distracted. It is better to give them movement activities related to the learning task, such as learning games, exercises, or simulations. Then they will be able to concentrate as well as people of other styles do when working in their element. Unless given productive activities related to their work, they will kick or swing their legs under the table, drum on the tabletop, slouch, rock in their seats, or find excuses to get up, whether it is to get a snack or look out the window.

Not all kinesthetic right-brain people are athletes. There are many other activities that involve movement. For them, movement can be moving in their mind from one topic or project to another.

Kinesthetic right-brain people can think about several things simultaneously and can have many projects going on at once. They can keep each one straight in their minds without any difficulty. They work in an impulsive, quick way, wanting to see results immediately so they can move on to another activity. In the rush to complete a project, they may not worry about whether the parts were done to perfection. They see the whole picture, not the details.

There are also times when they consider a job done just by having thought of it. Some kinesthetic right-brain people put the idea out, do some preliminary work, and move on to another project. It is up to the detail-oriented people around them to pick up the pieces and complete the task so they can then move on to create new inventions. They are a wealth of new ideas and discoveries, like a brainstorm session in motion, giving the world a seemingly endless supply of novel, unique ideas.

Being goal-oriented, kinesthetic right-brain people have the ability to get things done, handling many projects at once. They are not time-oriented, so they do not tend to stick to schedules, routines, or time constraints. They are go-with-the-flow people who will do what they feel like at the moment. They can keep work moving and be a wealth of creativity and imagination, although others have to be willing to accept their lack of consciousness of time. At work, as frequently as they arrive late, they may also become so absorbed in a task that they may stay overtime just to complete it.

A kinesthetic right-brain person needs a comfortable environment full of activity, with room to stretch out and move. Some will get up and leave if they are bored or in a restricted environment. Being outdoors is high on their list because there they can move freely.

Kinesthetic right-brain people enjoy being with other people when they can do something together that doesn't require a lot of talk. Watch them during a football game and you may hear grunts, moans, or cheers. They can communicate action without speaking and use their body and arms to dramatize or express what they want to describe. When they do talk, they use short action words and get to the point quickly.

Accelerated Learning

Kinesthetic right-brain people can accelerate their learning by moving in an unstructured, imaginative, and free-flowing way. They need to use their bodies and muscles to learn. Thus, they can learn better while cycling on a stationary bike, memorizing material while jumping rope, performing experiments, or playing creative games.

Kinesthetic right-brain people, often adventuresome and daring, enjoy challenges. They do not require step-by-step, detailed instructions. This group just needs to jump in and "do it." They pick up the how-to information by intuition or gut feelings and learn by trial and error, exploration, and discovery. They fully grasp the overall patterns of any situation and know what to do. Their excellent visual-spatial relations, intuition, and quick reflexes enable them to look at a problem, instantly judge a situation, and move accordingly, without words or written directions, to find the solution.

They are whole-to-part learners who need to see the big picture first and fill in the details later. For example, they will not give a detailed verbal account of a sports event—they will give the highlights and the winning score: the bottom line. If they see a whole math problem with the answer and several examples, they can figure out how to solve similar problems.

They listen better while in motion with their eyes focused down and away from the speaker. They remember more when they are in motion than when they are sitting still. When they are moving they can relax and concentrate.

Writing on a flip chart or an erasable board with large markers works better for them than writing while sitting. By involving their whole arm, legs, and body, they can put the activity into the kinesthetic realm. Making a mind map of material they need to know by using their whole arm to write provides more activity and helps them recall what they learned. They doodle not because of a tactile need to write but because it offers more movement than sitting still.

They need active real-life experiences or simulations. For example, when learning about accounting they would prepare a budget for a real company or an imaginary one they created for this learning experience. If volunteers are needed for a demonstration, kinesthetic right-brain learners jump at the chance to get out of their seats and do something. If they are learning a dance they will remember it not by watching someone else do it, but by doing it themselves. They need to fully immerse themselves in the experience in an unstructured way. Many of them do not want long explanations; they want to figure something out for themselves. They need teachers who will take on the role of a coach, use only key action words, and guide them if they ask for help.

If a situation does not permit the kinesthetic right-brain person to do an activity, their next resort is to watch activity on television, videos, or movies. To remember what they learn, they need to act out the material or visualize themselves dramatizing it as if a movie were playing in their head. When they visualize they need to feel movement in their muscles. Their body may move and sway as they go through the movements in their mind. When they receive directions to drive to a friend's house, they experience themselves turning the car right or left, or whipping along a curve in the road in their mind.

Good learning materials for a kinesthetic right-brain person are manipulatives, games, building materials, tools, sports equipment, balls, exercise bikes, large flip charts, erasable boards, large markers, computers with action games, percussion instruments, guitars or organs, rhythmic music, hands-on models, or real objects to move. They like unstructured, nonsequential, high-action, fast-moving video games and CD-ROM interactive programs. If a computer program is too slow or too structured, they become bored. They prefer moving a joystick or a mouse.

Competitions and challenges interest kinesthetic right-brain people, either in games or on the job. They may participate in contests that determine who can sell or produce the most. They are goal-oriented and enjoy the thrill of winning points for themselves or their team. Make a game of anything and they will learn it.

When they are studying for a test, they remember what they

did while learning. For them to concentrate, distractions caused by the movement of others have to be eliminated. Working in a study carrel, using a divider, or facing a wall can keep them from noticing the movement of others, but they have to be comfortable while studying. Being stretched out on the floor or couch gives their muscles freedom of movement. They can work and study with or without music. Because they do not listen to the words, it does not interfere with their reading. The rhythm or beat stimulates their muscles to move or dance in time to the music. Their stress is reduced and their attention and motivation increases.

By working in cooperative groups, kinesthetic right-brain learners have an opportunity to move around more from group to group. They thrive on change and interact with different people to satisfy their need for action.

To accelerate reading, kinesthetic right-brain people need to convert words into a movie in which they are part of the action. Imagining that they are directing a video and converting the book, or script, into scenes, describing the action that would appear on the screen, will make a book come alive for them. Whatever they do not feel themselves doing—or imagining they are doing—as they read will be lost to them.

They read for the main idea or big picture, skipping small details, and are impatient with too many words. Thus, they tend to miss comprehension questions that deal with details, time sequence, or abstract ideas. It is not that they cannot remember details, but they need kinesthetic right-brain techniques to master them.

Kinesthetic right-brain people prefer short or highly action-packed books or how-to books that help them perform better. Unlike their left-brain counterparts, they need diagrams, photographs, or illustrations. They do not like to read a book from cover to cover but tend to skip around, getting what they need from it. They may learn just by looking at the pictures, glancing at the captions, or flipping through the pages, catching stray sentences that may give them all they need to know about a topic. They have an intuitive sense that helps them find what they need.

Kinesthetic right-brain people need to know the end product

before they start. Thus, they need to know the reason they are reading something. They will be motivated if they feel it will help them do something better. Watch them zip through a book if they feel it will help them be the top in their field, boost their sales, or get a promotion. Books with summaries or key points at the beginning or end of a chapter help them find what is important and relevant to them.

In the workforce, they can be found in jobs that require movement and frequent change. They may not attend to details, but they will work quickly to get a job done rapidly. With this group, speed and completion takes priority over spending a great deal of time on detail, as long as the end product works. They can be involved in building, making, or fixing things such as cars, houses, boats, motorcycles, computers, appliances, machines, or furniture. They may do work that requires physical exertion such as construction, building bridges, or lifting boxes. Some work in jobs that require traveling, but with little talk. Long-distance driving, flying, chauffeuring, making deliveries, and trucking are good options for them if they are not constrained by time schedules. They may enjoy the adventure and risks involved in police work, fire fighting, or the armed forces. Many of them like to be self-employed so they do not have to follow someone else's schedule. They may run their own construction, painting, wallpapering, cleaning, moving, lawn maintenance, plumbing, electrical, or repair companies.

As scientists, kinesthetic right-brain people enjoy inventing, doing research and laboratory work, experimenting in the fields of paleontology, anthropology, quantum physics, or chemistry. If they go into medicine, they may run their own practices so they can have the freedom to set their own hours or move from one patient to another in ten different rooms.

They may be involved in dancing, gymnastics, track, skiing, skating, swimming, sailing, snorkeling, surfing, biking, gymnastics, Rollerblading, karate, judo, horseback riding, or aerobics. They may play football, soccer, tennis, and basketball for fun, but may have a hard time adjusting to being on an organized professional team because of the rigors of the schedule, discipline, and routine involved in that lifestyle.

Kinesthetic right-brain writers write short action stories that get to the point or how-to books that give key points without much detail. If they are artists they like art that requires action—huge canvasses or sculptures with strong movement of color and design. They tend to make quick, impressionistic drawings that give a general idea of what they are trying to say. If they are actors or actresses they may prefer to play action parts or be stunt people. If they are musicians they enjoy playing an instrument that allows them to move their bodies. Kinesthetic right-brain learners tend to be better at playing by ear than reading notes. They also tend to be imaginative and can come up with new tunes or forms of music.

Their imagination, new ideas, openness to change, and inventiveness make them an excellent resource. Their commitment to action makes them product-oriented and able to produce a large amount of work in a short amount of time. As they move, the world also moves forward in new directions.

Adapting Learning to a Kinesthetic Right-Brain Style

Kinesthetic right-brain learners need to ask an instructor to provide the big picture or overview using short, sensory language and let them do kinesthetic activities in a global, creative, free-flowing way. Since it is hard for them to follow auditory presentations, they need to have a written copy of notes or readings, or take dictation of a lecture and convert each word into a mental movie in which they play a part; a drawing with key words or numbers written in colorful, artistic, and creative ways; mind maps in color that show the main topic, the details, and their interconnections; or kinesthetic projects. They may need to find corresponding pictures, movies, or activities in which they can participate in real-life demonstrations. Instead of taking notes while sitting down, they can make the activity kinesthetic by writing and drawing in large letters or figures while standing up at a flip chart or board. They can convert information into a mind map that gives the big picture of the subject they are learning.

Accelerated Learning

18

A Step-by-Step Plan for Learning Anything Rapidly

You have now discovered your best learning link and are ready for this step-by-step plan to apply this knowledge to learn anything quickly. In Part 4 you will discover the ingredients for learning quickly using your best superlink. The six-step formula to rapid learning is:

- **Step 1: Planning:** In Chapter 19 you will plan your own program, beginning with the prelearning activities that will put you in the right frame of mind to learn quickly.
- **Step 2: Input:** In Chapter 20 you will find out what type of instruction, learning materials, and learning environment is needed to accelerate your learning.
- **Step 3: Comprehension:** In Chapter 21 you will find out how to increase your comprehension.
- **Step 4: Memory Improvement:** In Chapter 22 you will learn how to improve your memory to optimize learning.
- **Step 5: Note-Taking, Study Skills, and Test-Taking Skills:** In Chapter 23 you will learn how you can

improve your long-term memory by sharpening your note-taking, test-taking, and study skills.

- **Step 6: Application:** In Chapter 24 you will learn how to apply what you learned to your current situation.

The following section of the book is set up so that you can pick a subject you want to learn and use this guide to help you learn it. You may want to take notes and do the activities suggested for each chapter by writing in a notebook you've set aside for this purpose.

Select a subject you want to learn right away. The subject can be a course you are currently taking or a self-study program. It could be a topic you wish to learn about on your own or one that you will need to pass a test or qualifying exam, such as a GRE, SAT, or bar examination. It can be a skill you want to learn, such as using a computer program, building a deck, or playing golf. Many of the activities in this book lend themselves well to courses that require reading a textbook or listening to oral presentations, but the process can be applied equally well to learning a vocation, craft, sport, hobby, or a skill required on your job. Even in a performance task you need to receive information either from reading, listening, taking notes, doing something with your hands, or engaging your body. You will discover which method is the best for you no matter what the area in which you wish to learn.

Thus, as you continue on in this book, you will be learning two things: how to learn anything quickly, and the *subject* that you want to learn quickly. Once you master these techniques you can use them for any other subject or field you wish to learn throughout the rest of your life.

EXERCISE: Select the subject, topic, or skill you want to learn.

19

Preparation

You are now ready to begin the process of accelerated learning. Ask yourself the following questions before you get started:

- What is my motivation, purpose, or goal for learning this subject?
- What do I already know about this subject?
- What do I need to know about this subject?
- What is the best way for me to learn?
- How can I raise my self-esteem and use positive thinking about myself?
- What are some relaxation and stress reduction techniques to optimize learning?
- How can I visualize success?

What Is My Motivation, Purpose, or Goal for Learning This Subject?

People remember things that serve a purpose in their lives. Every day we are bombarded with information that we see, hear, smell, taste, or touch, but we only remember what we consider important, otherwise we would be unable to sort through the multitude of stimuli we receive.

Our brain has the decision-making capacity to sort out what is relevant. Whatever it decides to remember, it will remember. This is a choice we make continually and is something we should keep in mind when learning. As information is conveyed to us we can observe it passively and let it bounce off us, or we can take it in and retain it. Think about several subjects you have learned throughout your life. Were there times when you attended a lecture or read a book, hearing and seeing the words, but moments later the information was gone? You did not really *learn* the material—you did not commit it to memory. Were there other times when you decided that you really needed to remember the information you received, so you paid close attention to it, absorbed it, and remembered it? Somehow, you made a decision to remember it because you had an important reason for doing so, whether you wanted to excel at your job or had an important test to pass. Whatever the reason, your learning increased because you were motivated to learn.

Motivation to learn is a key ingredient in presetting your mind for learning. If you take a few seconds at the start of any learning session and say, "What is my purpose or goal in learning this material?" you will have programmed your mind to be attentive and interested. The more relevant the subject is to your life, the greater chance you have for keeping your attention fully on the subject.

Determine why you need to learn the subject you selected, and keep this goal in mind as you learn the new material.

EXERCISE: Write down your reason for learning this subject.

What Do I Already Know About the Subject?

The next step in the planning stage of your learning is to evaluate what you already know about the subject. To accelerate your learning you'll need to fit the instruction into the shortest possible time. One way to do this is to eliminate wasting time relearning what you already know. You want to focus on new information.

To make this evaluation, write down what you already know about the subject. Only list what you are sure that you know because you may need a refresher for some material. As you go through your learning program you can skip or skim over what you already know to save time.

EXERCISE: Write down what you already know about the subject you've chosen to learn.

What Do I Need to Know About This Subject?

After determining what you already know, the next step is to evaluate what you *need* to know about the subject. Most people go blindly into a subject. They plod along from one point to the next, starting at the front cover of a book and ending at the back. If the book contains topics that are not relevant, you should skip them to avoid being slowed down.

If you take a course, you will probably be guided by an instructor who will tell you what you need to learn. If you are doing a self-study program, you need to do some preparation in advance and find out what you want to know about the subject. Do you want to master a certain process or skill and cover certain topics? Do you want to show proficiency in one area or know everything that was ever written about that subject? Decide what it is you need to know to satisfy your goals. List those topics and use the list as your guide. In this way you can select the most helpful material and skip what is irrelevant to your learning plan.

EXERCISE: Write down what you need to know about the subject.

What Is the Best Way for Me to Learn?

You already discovered your superlink, an important ingredient in the entire learning process. Using methods that are compatible with your superlink can be a key factor in determining how successfully and quickly you will learn the subject. By using the right learning materials you accelerate learning by eliminating unnecessary barriers that can slow learning down.

EXERCISE: Review the information on your superlink and list the best learning methods and materials for you.

How Can I Use Positive Thinking to Accelerate Learning?

If you had a hard time learning in school, you may not have enough confidence in yourself and your abilities. Perhaps you saw others earn high grades while you got low grades or even failed. Unfortunately, this kind of negative attitude becomes a self-fulfilling prophecy. When we think we can't do something we put so much energy into that negative thought that we end up not succeeding. On the other hand, when we think we can succeed we work with confidence and end up succeeding.

One study conducted by Harvard researchers, led by Robert Rosenthal, and that later became known as "Pygmalion in the Classroom," focused on a group of ninety students of average ability. Three teachers to whom they were assigned in classes of thirty each were told that they were gifted students. The teachers, thinking that they had gifted students, taught them as if they *were* gifted and had high expectations of them. At the end of the study the progress of each group was measured. The results were that the students met those expectations, did exceedingly well, and their achievement soared.* What this study points out is that our performance can be influenced by our expectations of ourselves as well as others' expectations of us.

You may have been slowed down because you were not taught in your learning style. You learned quickly in the first few years of life because you were allowed to use your natural way of learning— the learning method that is easiest for you—watching, listening, exploring, playing learning games, or any other method. But in traditional schools students must learn in one or two ways, by watching

*Canter, Lee, and Canter, Marlene. *The High Performing Teacher: Avoiding Burnout and Increasing Your Motivation.* A Publication of Lee Canter and Associates. Santa Monica, CA. 1994, pp. 25–26.

(a visual method) and listening (an auditory one) to the teacher. If students do not have the same learning style as the one used in the classroom they struggle to learn. The amount of time they spend trying to adapt to a learning style that is not their strongest is time taken away from learning. Thus, while they struggle to grasp a lesson presented in a learning style that is not compatible with their own, the class has already moved on. These students do not know what is wrong with them or why others are getting it and they are not. They do not know that if they were taught in a learning style that matched their own they would move along as quickly as some of the other students. But the students do not know what to ask for. They are prisoners of a system that is not working for them.

If you are one of those who experienced failure or felt you could not learn as quickly as others, or were a good student and wanted to be better and could not, you were probably just as bright as those other children but were limited by a learning method that was not compatible with your own. The students who did well may have been those whose superlink matched the teacher's presentation. If you were to take those who did well and put them in a learning environment that is incompatible with their learning style, they also might fail.

You need to start a cycle of success. How is this done? First, think of a time when you succeeded at a task. It could have been a school subject, an extracurricular activity, or something you did on your own at home. Try to relive the experience in your mind. How did it feel to succeed? Did you feel happy, proud, and confident? Did you want to repeat the experience? Most people would say they would like to repeat the task because of the good feelings that accompanied the experience.

Now think of a time when you failed at something. It could have been a school subject, a sport or hobby, or something you did at home. How did you feel? Did you feel hurt, angry, frustrated, stupid, or hopeless? Did you want to repeat that task again? Most people, unless they wanted to repeat it just to prove to themselves they could do it, would say they would not want to repeat the task. Thus, because of the pain of the experience, they began to avoid the very area in which they may have needed to practice. The more they avoided practicing, the further they grew from mastering it. The cycle of failure began. The initial failure caused them to avoid the task, get further behind, and reinforced more failure.

It is time to break the cycle. By learning according to your best learning link you will now find it easier to learn. Gain confidence. Start with some easy work to regain the good feelings that come with success. Then, as you find you can finally succeed, slowly add harder and more challenging material. Do not frustrate yourself by beginning with material that is too hard. Until you regain your self-esteem, master the technique of learning in your best learning link using some review material. Then add new material as you regain confidence.

Whatever your level of education, know that you carry in your head a most remarkable computer. You just have to fit compatible software into the hardware of your brain for it to run properly. Many others who have tried these methods have succeeded, and you can too!

EXERCISE: Tell yourself, "I can raise my self-esteem and think positive thoughts about myself by realizing the possible causes of my previous struggles with learning." List subjects with which you previously had trouble, analyze how they were taught and how the methods may not have been compatible with your best learning style. List methods compatible with your learning link that could have been used to make those subjects easier to learn.

Why Are Relaxation and Stress Reduction Techniques Important?

Relaxation and stress reduction can accelerate learning. Medical research over the past decade has been exploring the connection between mind and body. When we are in a state of fear or extreme stress, the body's survival reaction is to shut down our thinking portion and respond according to the part of the brain that deals with the fight-or-flight response. We respond with physiological reactions such as increases of adrenaline, rapid heartbeats, and constricted blood vessels. Your body is readying itself to run or fight, requiring the use of your arms and legs. During this state you are not ready to remember a mathematical theorem or new vocabulary words.

People who had negative experiences of failure in the class-room enter into this state of panic and fear when it comes to learning. Their teachers or parents may have been upset with them, inflicted physical, psychological, or emotional pain and punishment, called them demeaning names, or ostracized them because of their mistakes at school. Years of reliving this trauma may cause people to enter a state of stress, panic, and fear when they have to learn something new. For successful learning to take place we need to learn how to relax and reduce stress. We have to program ourselves to break the cycle of failure and get out of the habit of fearing learning. Relaxation and stress-reduction techniques can assist in the process.

The first step is to put the past behind you, realize that these struggles were not entirely your fault, and remind yourself that the fear response is only a habit. You now know what you need in order to learn; things *will* be different this time. By following a new approach that suits your style, you will be more success-ful. So relax—this time you *will* succeed!

Step two is to get your body into a physiological state of re-laxation. Our brain waves run at different frequencies. From thir-teen to twenty Hz (Hertz), or cps (cycles per second), we are in the beta state, the state in which we function at work, driving, or in the fight-or-flight mode. From eight to twelve Hz we are in the alpha state, in which we are more relaxed, but alert. The alpha state is good for learning. The theta state, from four to eight Hz, is the meditation state. This is good for relaxation and stress re-duction. From one to four Hz we are in the delta state, which is deep sleep. Before learning we may want to reduce our stress and increase our relaxation by entering into the theta state—the state of meditation. There are different ways to do this.

One way to reach the state of relaxation is to slow down our breathing. In fear, the hormones we release increase our heart rate. To reduce a rapid heart rate and to relax, find a place to sit in a relaxed position. Take some deep breaths, letting the air fill your lungs. Breathe to the count of four, hold for four, and release your breath in four. Do this slow breathing for several minutes, until you feel your heartbeat slow down. As you breathe in, feel a light enter you, filling your entire body. Imagine this light filling you with relaxation. Feel your stress evaporate and the light fill you with calm and peace instead. Imagine that this light is bringing with it a wisdom and knowledge that will help you learn anything you want to know. You can then feel the stress of your body disappear and relaxation fill you up.

Another way to get to the theta state is to still your mind and eliminate all thoughts of panic, worry, and fear. Sitting for a few minutes in meditation calms your mind. You can close your eyes in a relaxed manner. Concentrate on the field of darkness lying in front of you as if you were watching a movie screen, or looking into the dark night sky. Sit in a relaxed manner, looking into the center of what is in front of you. Do not think about anything, just look into the middle of the field of vision. Your mind will become concentrated and focused. A feeling of relaxation will come over your body and mind. By keeping your attention on one point you will find your powers of concentration become focused and sharp. You may feel a sense of peace. Some people even get a feeling of blissful joy. Your worries and fears melt away—you are now in the state where you are ready to learn.

Some people try a variety of other techniques for relaxation. Some use music to get into this state. Early work with accelerated learning developed by the Bulgarian researcher Georgi Lozanov relied on music to get the mind ready for learning. Baroque music, which contains sixty beats per minute, supposedly synchronizes with the heartbeat, helping people get into an optimal learning state.

More recently, musician Steven Halpern has found that music with less than sixty beats per minute also works. His research reveals that music with a slower beat slows the heart rate, putting the body and mind into a more relaxed state, ideal for learning. He has been a pioneer in producing music to accelerate learning. Some schools have used his music to create a calm, peaceful state in which students can learn in a stress-free attitude.

Some people like to do physical exercise or yoga to get the body relaxed. Exercise or physical yoga stimulates the flow of oxygen through the bloodstream, carrying it to the brain to eliminate mental stress and get the brain ready for learning.

Whatever method you use, the end result is to calm the body and mind to keep them out of the fight or flight mode. Before beginning a learning session, spend five or ten minutes in any of the relaxation techniques. You can do the same one every day, or you can vary them. Find those that work the best for you. The goal is to keep the higher-thinking functions in the brain open so that learning can take place.

EXERCISE: Try the different *stress-reduction* activities to find those that are best for you.

How Can I Visualize Success?

The last step in the planning stage for learning is to visualize success. Athletes have been using this technique for years. Before a competition, they visualize or imagine themselves winning. The power of a positive mental mind-set is used in other fields as well. Medical researchers and doctors have reported cases in which after the visualization of good health their patients' health improved. Health centers around the world have been established, devoted to helping people visualize themselves becoming healthy. The same technique has been used for increasing learning.

The technique is simple. Sit quietly in a relaxed state. You can get into a meditative state first so that the body and mind are calm and stilled.

For Visual Learners: Picture yourself successfully completing the course in whatever subject you are trying to learn.

For Auditory Learners: Hear yourself say that you have successfully completed the course.

For Tactile Learners: Feel the joy of success of completing the course.

For Kinesthetic Learners: Experience yourself jumping up and giving a victory punch with your fist into the air and saying, "Yes!" after successfully completing the course.

Try to make the image of your successful moment as vivid as possible, using all your senses. Be actively engaged in some action as a result of your successful learning. Live the successful moment as if it really has already happened. Repeat this activity daily. Know that you have already succeeded. Live each day as one more step leading to the success that is already yours. Students have successfully used this technique to win scholarships or admission into schools in which the competition is fierce.

Visualizing your success as well as doing the steps in this accelerated program go hand in hand. The visualization of success adds the power of positive thinking to the tools you are learning. You are now ready to learn the subject you have chosen to master.

EXERCISE: Visualize yourself succeeding at learning the subject you chose and write a description of what you visualized.

20

Instruction, Materials, and Learning Environment

After preparing your mind for optimum learning, you are ready to begin taking in the information you need to learn. You should consider:

- how instruction should be delivered to fit your learning link and the learning materials you should use
- the learning environment you need
- how to convert information from your weaker style to your best style

You want to choose the type of instruction, learning materials, and learning environment that will allow you to absorb information that matches your superlink in order to learn more rapidly.

If you have control over your learning plan, you can make the above decisions about the type of instruction yourself. In many cases, though, you will be learning from others, either through a course, a required manual, or a curriculum prescribed for your training in your field of work. Some of the above decisions may not rest in your hands, but are left up to the instructor or the institution preparing your learning program. The people teaching you may not do so in a way that matches your best learning link. In that case, you have two options. The first option is to explain to the instructor or coordinator of your studies how you learn best and ask him or her to present the material in a way that is compatible with your learning style. The second option comes into play when the instructor or coordinator does not want to or cannot present the material in your best style. In that case you need to learn how to convert the type of instruction to your own best learning link. This chapter will teach you how to do this. This ability can be a powerful tool that will enable you to learn in *any* situation— you won't need to rely on others to determine whether or not you succeed.

Fit the Instruction to Your Learning Link

There are many ways to learn a subject. The medium is the communication method used to convey the material. Below are some of the different instructional media:

Written Material: books, textbooks, manuals, guidebooks, booklets, pamphlets, reference materials such as encyclopedias, almanacs, dictionaries, or thesauruses, magazines, journals, newspapers, microfilm, microfiche, scripts, screenplays, poetry, charts, lists, diagrams, and graphs.

Graphic Material: photographs, illustrations, pictures, drawings, maps, atlases, posters, cartoons, and diagrams and charts with graphics.

Audio-Visual Material: cassette tapes, CD's, slides, filmstrips, movies, videotapes, radio, television, and teleconferencing.

From Computer: software programs, CD-ROM, virtual reality, E-mail, and on-line services such as the Worldwide Web, Internet, Prodigy, and America On-Line.

Hands-On Activities: writing, typing, drawing, sketching, painting, sculpting, carpentry, construction, arts and crafts, role-playing games, simulations, learning games, using manipulatives, dramatization, film-making, video production, theatrical and musical production, demonstrations, making discoveries, exploration, performing experiments, sports, and exercise.

Real-Life Experiences: on-the-job training, fieldwork, trips to museums, learning centers (such as oceanariums, forest preserves, environmental centers), farms, construction sites, power plants, stores, hospitals, schools, factories, post offices, or any other applicable location.

Personal Instructors: teachers, professors, guides, mentors, coaches, facilitators, trainers, skilled craftspeople, employers, managers, or supervisors.

Combinations of the Above: Any of the above teaching methods can be combined.

Based on the description of your learning link that you read in Part 3 of the book, choose the medium from the above lists that corresponds with your superlink. For example, if you are a visual right-brain person, the medium you need would be graphic material, movies, videos, printed material written in a visual right-brain style, or real-life experiences.

If you can control your learning, then you can set it up in the way that will help you learn quickly. But we do not always have control over the way we are instructed. We may not be in charge of choosing the best medium or learning material, or selecting the learning environment. Is learning hopeless? Not at all. What you can do is to convert any instruction into your own best style. You can still learn even if the medium, material, *and* environment do not suit your style. The following chart will enable you to convert any information into the style that best suits your superlink. Think of it as a translation system to show you what you can do to turn a poor situation into an optimal one.

Converting Instruction Into Your Learning Link

On the left side of the chart below, find your best learning link. Across the top are listed the different media through which information is conveyed. Where the two intersect, instructions are given, wherever necessary, on how to convert a medium or some aspect of it into the best medium for your superlink.

Media

Learning Link	Written Material	Graphic Material	Audio-Visual Material	Computers	Hands-on Activities	Real-life Experience	Learning from an Instructor
Visual Left-Brain	Ideal for visual left-brain learners	Label and describe the graphic material.	Use a study guide or script or take notes to review later.	Read a manual or take notes when graphics are the only displayed programs.	Read the directions for the activity or write your own.	Refer to a written description of the activity.	If the presentation is auditory, tactile, or kinesthetic make your own outline, directions, or study guide to read later.
Visual Right-Brain	Draw pictures and diagrams to accompany the text.	Ideal for visual right-brain learners	For written text, or audio media without graphics, create your own sketches or graphic material.	For programs with written text, draw your own illustrations, graphic images, or mind maps to accompany the text.	Make an illustrated instruction booklet for the activity.	Take notes on the experience and illustrate them.	If the instruction is auditory, tactile, or kinesthetic, take notes by drawing sketches or graphic images of the material.
Auditory Left-Brain	Read the material aloud and discuss it.	Talk about the material and discuss it with others.	Ideal for auditory left-brain learners. For visual media without sound, talk about the material with others.	Read aloud any text that appears on the screen.	Talk about the activities while doing them and get step-by-step directions.	Talk about the activities while doing them and get step by step directions.	For a visual, tactile, or kinesthetic presentation, ask questions, discuss, describe the process, read aloud what you wrote, or verbally describe the moves step-by-step.

Learning Link	Written Material	Graphic Material	Audio-Visual Material	Computers	Hands-on Activities	Real-life Experience	Learning from an Instructor
Auditory Right-Brain	Make a mental movie of the material, visualizing color, sound, feeling, and action, or invent rhymes, raps, songs, or poetry about the material.	Create rhymes, raps, songs, or poetry to help you remember the material; discuss material with others.	Ideal for auditory left-brain learners. For visual media without sound, add your own sound effects.	Add graphics and sound effects to written text and read aloud with others.	For visual, tactile, or kinesthetic activities: Make a mind map. Add sound, sound effects, music, and talk about them.	For visual, tactile, or kinesthetic real-life experiences: Make a mind map; Add sound, sound effects, music, and talk about them with others.	For a visual, tactile, or kinesthetic presentation: Convert it into a movie in your mind using all your senses; make a mind map and add sound, sound effects, music, and talk about it with others; use associations, mnemonics, poetry, raps, rhymes, or songs.
Tactile Left-Brain	Copy material in your own hand or type it.	Write a description of the graphics in your own hand, type it, or make a model.	Take notes.	For graphics, write descriptions in your own hand or type them out.	Ideal for tactile left-brain learners. Use a step-by-step approach and put it into words.	For visual, auditory, and kinesthetic activities, take notes and involve feelings.	For visual, auditory, and kinesthetic instruction, take notes, do hands-on activities, and involve feelings.
Tactile Right-Brain	Draw, sketch, or make graphics to illustrate the words.	Copy or draw the visuals or do a hands-on activity related to it; involve feelings.	Draw, sketch, diagram, or do a hands-on activity related to the audio-visual materials.	Convert the written text from computers into graphics.	Ideal for right-brain learners. Use a global approach.	Make sketches to remind you of the experience.	Make sketches or pictorial diagrams of the presentation.
Kinesthetic Left-Brain	Act out the words or visualize the action in your mind in a step-by-step way.	Physically act out the graphic representation or visualize the action in your mind in a step-by-step way.	Dramatize or visualize the action sequentially.	Physically act out the written text or graphics on computers or visualize the action in a step-by-step way.	Visual, auditory, and tactile activities: need to be carried out physically, or visualize the action in a step-by-step way, putting it into words.	Ideal for kinesthetic left-brain learners. Use as a step-by-step approach and put it into words.	For visual, auditory, and tactile presentations: need to be carried out physically, or visualize the action in a step-by-step way, putting it into words.

Learning Link	Written Material	Graphic Material	Audio-Visual Material	Computers	Hands-on Activities	Real-life Experience	Learning from an Instructor
Kinesthetic Right-Brain	Physically act out the words or visualize the action in your mind.	Physically act out the graphic representation or visualize the action in your mind.	Carry out physically, or visualize the action.	Written text or graphics on computers need to be physically carried out; or visualize the action with freedom of movement and imagination.	Visual, auditory, and tactile activities: Participate in the experience, or visualize the action with freedom of movement and imagination.	Ideal for kinesthetic right-brain learners. Use a global approach.	Visual, auditory, and tactile instruction, need to physically act out or visualize the action with freedom of movement and imagination.

Each type of learning material can be made suitable for any type of learner. There is no reason for books and graphic materials to be made only for visual people. Books can be written to appeal to auditory, tactile, and kinesthetic people who are either left-brain or right-brain or both. As a consultant and a writer of learning materials, I develop programs that deliver instruction through the medium that matches the learners. Any medium can be converted to match the learner's style.

EXERCISE: Go through the chapter on your superlink and the media chart, your best medium of instruction. Take notes of all the media that match your best learning link. Remember, if you are a combination of learning links, select media from different columns, since you have two or more best learning links.

Then, use the information provided in the chart "The Learning Environment You Need," to list the coping skills you will use to convert them into your learning link. Again, if you are a combination of learning links, select coping strategies from all the columns that apply to you.

Apply the information in the chart to an actual learning experience.

The Learning Environment You Need

Your learning environment refers to where you will work, read, or study: the conditions in the room and the other stimuli that can enhance or inhibit your ability to learn. You may have set yourself up with the right delivery of instruction and the right materials, but if your environment causes you discomfort or distractions it will be harder to concentrate. To accelerate learning you want to eliminate as many steps that block your progress as possible.

When you set up your own environment, you can control your circumstances. But when you are in a training or class situation, you may not have control over your environment. Thus, you may have to ask the instructor for some assistance in making some adjustments in the environment, or use coping techniques to help you adapt to the situation. Below is a list summarizing the best learning environment for each superlink, followed by coping skills for adapting a noncompatible environment into one that is compatible for you.

Superlink	Best Learning Environment	Coping Strategies to Adapt a Noncompatible Environment
Visual Left-Brain Learners	• Written material and the speaker are clearly visible • No visual clutter or disorganization • Printed material is neat and free of errors. • Can work with or without music or auditory distractions because they are not auditorially attuned. • Room is complete with filing systems, visual organizers, time schedules, calendars, and clocks. • The instructor arrives on time and finishes on time.	• Try to sit close to the front. • Keep your own area neat and organized. Offer to clean up, organize, and decorate the rest of the room. • Correct errors in printed material. • Request a time schedule. Wear a watch. Offer to be a timekeeper.
Visual Right-Brain Learners	• Graphic or written material and the speaker are clearly visible. • Visually attractive, colorful, and creative environment. • Comfortable seats and chairs. • Flexible schedule allows you to come and go at varying times.	• Sit near the front. • Keep your own area colorful, well designed, and attractive. • Offer to decorate the area of the room you have to look at. • Select a comfortable seat, or bring a cushion or pillow to make it more comfortable. • Use a color-coded, decorative calendar to artistically track your deadlines. Put up sticky-note messages to attract your attention and remind you of deadlines and due dates.
Auditory Left-Brain Learners	• You can listen to others and discuss your own ideas. • Only one auditory stimulus at a time. • No music in background while studying or reading. • Silence for reading or studying. • Orderly environment has filing systems, organizers, and time schedules. • The speaker is clearly audible. • Instructor gives out schedules, comes on time, and leaves on time.	• Sit with someone who will discuss the topic with you. • Sit where you can hear the speaker. Stay away from areas with noise distraction. • Bring a headphone or earplugs to tune out music or distracting sounds when reading or studying. • If you need to talk to yourself or read aloud, sit in an area where you will not disturb others. (Most likely the only ones who will be disturbed are other auditory people.) • Ask for a time schedule. Wear a watch.

Superlink	Best Learning Environment	Coping Strategies to Adapt a Noncompatible Environment
Auditory Right-Brain Learners	• The sounds in the environment are pleasant. • Sounds are harmonious with one another, for example, music combined with natural sounds. • Talk is kept to a minimum, with key points emphasized. • Comfortable seats. • Flexible time schedule. • Speaker is clearly audible. • Absolute quiet for studying. • No music in background while studying or reading.	• Listen to music while doing work that does not require abstract thinking in the form of words. • Sit where you can hear the speaker and stay away from areas with noise distraction. • Sit with someone who can repeat key points and verbal directions slowly and repeatedly, if needed, until you understand them. • Sit in a comfortable seat, or bring a cushion or pillow to make uncomfortable seats feel better. • Keep a color-coded calendar or use sticky-notes as reminders of time. • Bring headphones or earplugs to tune out distractions.
Tactile Left-Brain Learners	• Environment is physically and emotionally comfortable. • You can sit next to people you like. • You know the schedule and can see a clock. • Room is organized and neat. • You are permitted to write, draw, and doodle as you listen or read. • Can work with or without music you like. • Instructor with positive communication style.	• Sit in a comfortable seat, or bring a cushion or pillow to make uncomfortable seats feel better. • If you do not like air-conditioning or heat, sit far from the ventilators or blowers. If you do not like sun glare, avoid sitting in the line of sunlight. If you like sun, or need greenery or a peaceful view, sit near the window. • Select a location where you feel emotionally comfortable. Sit near people you like. • Ask for a time schedule. Wear a watch. • Keep an organizer for your papers. • Keep notepaper and pens available. Sit where doodling, writing, or touching objects does not bother the instructor or others. • If you need music, bring headphones.

Superlink	Best Learning Environment	Coping Strategies to Adapt a Noncompatible Environment
Tactile Right-Brain Learners	• Comfortable seats. (Some may like to stretch out on the floor, sit on a desktop, or recline or stretch out in their seats.) • Physically comfortable environment. • You can sit near people you like and far away from people who do not like you. • You are allowed to doodle, draw, or sketch. • You can work with or without music, but it needs to be music you like. • Flexible schedule. • Instructor is someone you like and admire.	• Select your own seating to be physically and emotionally comfortable. Bring a pillow or cushion if the seat is uncomfortable. • If you like scenery, sit near a window. Sit near or away from heaters, air-conditioners, or sun glare, depending on comfort level. • Sit near someone you like. Avoid sitting near people who make you feel uncomfortable or upset. • Keep drawing paper, pens, or markers for doodling and sketching, and sit where this does not distract others. • If you like music to keep you feeling relaxed and positive, bring headphones so as not to disturb others. • Keep a color-coded calendar or use sticky-notes as reminders of time. • Keep objects or belongings that make you feel good on your desk or table. Give your desk or area a personal touch.
Kinesthetic Left-Brain Learners	• Plenty of space to stretch out or move around. • You can get out of your seat or work standing up. • Comfortable seats. • Boards or flip charts allow you to stand up and write. • Neat, organized surroundings. • Time schedules.	• Sit near the back of the room so you can move around without distracting anyone. • Bring a cushion or pillow to make uncomfortable seats feel better. • Wear a watch to keep track of the time. Ask for a schedule. • Bring a challenging game or activity or something to do quietly at your seat when you get bored. • If you like music, bring headphones. • Do arm or leg exercises at your seat if you get bored. • When studying, sit in a study carrel or put up a book or divider to block out the distraction of others' movements.

Superlink	Best Learning Environment	Coping Strategies to Adapt a Noncompatible Environment
Kinesthetic Right-Brain Learners	• Enough space to move around and stretch out. • You can get out of your seat or work standing up. • Room has comfortable seating or places to sit or stretch out on the floor. • You can play learning or movement games. • You are permitted to work with or without music. • You can look out the window or, when studying, sit at a study carrel or have a divider to block out the view of others' activities. • Boards or flip charts allow you to stand up and write. • You are permitted to arrive late, leave early when your work is done, or work well past the finishing time.	• Select a place where you can move around without disturbing others, preferably at the back of the room. • Make sure your seat is comfortable; bring cushions or pillows. • Bring a challenging game or activity, or something to do quietly when bored. • If you like music, listen to it using headphones while learning. • Sit at a study carrel or use a book or divider to block out distractions from others' movements. • Keep a color-coded calendar or use sticky-notes as reminders of time.

EXERCISE: Use some of the above suggestions for your super-link in your next learning session.

21

Comprehension

In Chapter 20 you learned how to receive information in the fastest, most natural manner through your superlink. The next step is to ensure that you comprehend the material. Think of it as having a delivery person get past the checkpoints in a high-security building. Using the best and fastest route, he delivers the letter. The next question is: Do you understand what the message says? Understanding the message is called comprehension.

We may have material conveyed to us through our best learning style, but without training we still may not comprehend it. Or we may comprehend only a portion of it. Comprehension is a skill that can be learned. Think back to a test you did not do well on, as painful as the memory may be. Did you study really hard only to score seventy-five percent, eighty-eight percent, or even way below sixty-five percent? What happened? You only comprehended a portion of the material you learned. You thought you studied hard. What was missing? You may not have learned the skill of comprehension.

In many schools today we continue to test students' comprehension. If they fail, we have them study again, retest them and see what they score the second or third time around. But do we teach them *how* to comprehend? We often think that comprehension is a genetically-transmitted trait that we are born with or that we pick up by osmosis. It is not: It is a learned, acquired skill. In this chapter you will learn the secrets to increasing your comprehension, and hopefully it won't remain secret anymore. From first grade up to college and at the adult level, everyone needs to learn how to comprehend, but many adults never learned this at all. So get ready for Comprehension Made Easy 101!

Comprehension Techniques
for the Eight Superlinks

By now you have an idea that people with different learning styles and brain hemispheric preferences think differently, remember differently, and respond to the world in a different way. They also comprehend in a different manner. The following are reading comprehension techniques I have developed and used successfully with people of all learning styles and brain hemispheric preferences. If you use these techniques your comprehension can improve drastically. Many people who were previously struggling with comprehension have became so successful through the use of these techniques that they can actually comprehend one hundred percent of what they read. If this were taught in schools from first grade on, we would see higher achievement rates for all students and adults. For those who are good readers, you may already intuitively know how to comprehend everything you read. But there are millions of adults who struggle with reading. They may pick up the gist of what they read, but miss most of it. The exercise in this section is designed to sharpen your comprehension if you are a good reader and can also help millions of adults who managed to make it through school—or even through graduate school—but who wished they had known a way to read better and comprehend more fully. Many adults who have successful careers are still not satisfied with their ability to fully comprehend and remember what they read. They feel they have to take a long time to make it through readings and do not recall what they read. Overwhelmed by the many professional journals or training materials they are required to read at the workplace, they are too embarrassed to tell anyone about their struggle or to seek help. This chapter provides some tools to make reading easier for those who want to learn more quickly and easily but who have been slowed down by poor comprehension techniques.

The basic technique for comprehension, which I have named "experiential" or "virtual reality" comprehension, will be described below, followed by adaptations for the different learning links.

INSTRUCTIONS: To begin this exercise, you will read a sample passage, phrase by phrase. You are going to imagine that you are a movie director and are going to convert the words into a movie or video. Your job is to set up the scene, guide the actors and actresses as to what they should be doing and what their facial expressions should be, control the sound, and direct the action. Pretend that the printed text is a screenplay you have to convert back into action. Did you ever realize that printed text is merely a transcription of imaginary or real-life events that have been converted into words so that those who were not on the spot could read it to find out what happened? Reading is converting words back into the actual experience or ideas that the author is trying to convey. So that is your job as a movie director—convert the words back into a movie. The following adaptations will be made by people with each learning link.

Visual Experiential Comprehension—Left and Right Brain: As you read, you will imagine yourself *seeing* a movie on a screen. You will watch this movie in your mind, seeing the people, places, and things. The question to ask yourself after reading each phrase or sentence is: "What am I *seeing* in this movie?"

Visual left-brain people will attend more to the visual language described, the sequence of events, and the linear structure of what they are reading.

Visual-right brain people will visualize the colors, shapes, sizes, designs, and patterns. They will see the expressions on people's faces.

Auditory Experiential Comprehension—Left and Right Brain: As you read, you will imagine yourself *listening* to the movie and *hearing* the dialogue and voices, sounds, and sound effects. You can also be the one reading the lines or carrying on the discussions. After reading each phrase or sentence the question to ask yourself is: "What am I *hearing*, what *sounds* am I making, or what am I *saying* in my movie?"

Auditory left-brain people will hear the words of the movie in their heads and get meaning from them with or without the images.

Auditory right-brain people will listen to the music and sound effects they create to go with the movie. You will hear the sounds of the words, tones of voice, environmental sounds, musical background, and accompaniment.

Tactile Experiential Comprehension—Left and Right Brain: As you read, you will imagine yourself *feeling* the events of the movie as if they were happening to you. You will immerse yourself in the characters and feel their emotions. You will feel the sensation of touch on your skin as if you were there. The question to ask yourself after reading each phrase or sentence is: "What am I *feeling* in my movie?"

Tactile left-brain people will pay more attention to feelings and emotions that are expressed in words.

Tactile right-brain people will be more attuned to descriptions of nonverbal communication and emotions experienced inferentially—implied by the words.

Kinesthetic Experiential Comprehension—Left and Right Brain: As you read, you will imagine yourself experiencing the action or doing the movement described in the movie. Either watch the action or become the actors or actresses and carry out the movements yourself. Make the movie come alive. The question to ask yourself after reading each phrase or sentence is: "What am I *doing* or *experiencing* in my movie?"

Kinesthetic left-brain people will be more attuned to the action words used.

Kinesthetic right-brain people will use their imaginations to act out the movie. They will convert everything into some movement they can feel their muscles make.

Sample Passage: "Rapid Learning"

Now let's learn how to use the experiential comprehension technique. Below is a sample passage, but *do not* read it until the instructions tell you to do so. For the moment skip down to below the passage and read it according to "How to Read the Sample Passage 'Rapid Learning.'" This exercise will teach you how to read using full experiential comprehension.

An eager young man desired a part-time job to help make his way through Stanford University. As he stood before Louis Janin one Friday morning, he was told there was only a stenographer position available. "I'd love it!" exclaimed the excited young man. "However, I can't start until next Wednesday."

Bright and early on Wednesday morning, the young man reported for duty.

"I like the promptness and enthusiasm," Janin assured the lad. "I do have one question. Why couldn't you start on Monday?"

"Well, you see, sir, I had to find a typewriter and learn how to use it," replied the young man—Herbert Hoover— who would become president of the United States.[1]

How to Read the Sample Passage "Rapid Learning"

Read the first few words of the passage, "An eager young man." Either with your eyes opened or closed, ask yourself, "What am I seeing (hearing or saying, feeling, or experiencing) on my movie

---

[1]From *The Speaker's Sourcebook: Quotes, Stories, and Anecdotes for Every Occasion,* by Glenn Van Ekeren N.J.: Prentice Hall, 1988), 382–83.

screen now?" Think of this as the opening scene of the movie. The first thing that will appear is "a young man." Since you are the director, imagine a man in your mind, any way you want, unless the passage describes him specifically. Some of you may visualize a tall man, a thin man, and so forth. Unless, or until, the passage describes the man, imagine him any way you can. Now, let's work on "eager." Visual people may see an expression of eagerness on his face. Auditory people may hear eagerness in his voice. Tactile people may feel eagerness themselves. Kinesthetic people may feel their body moving forward physically expressing eagerness.

Now, read the next group of words: "desired a part-time job to make his way through Stanford University." Ask yourself, "What am I seeing (hearing or saying, feeling, or doing) on my movie screen now?" Then describe to yourself what appears on the screen. Some of you may see a college student carrying books and rushing off after school to a small office. Auditory learners may hear him say to his college friends, "I have to get a job to pay for school," and then hear the sound of the car radio blasting as he drives to work." Tactiles may feel the anxiety of needing a part-time job to make money to pay the bills. Kinesthetics may experience hopping in their car to drive to a part-time job, racing through streets, feeling the sensation of steering the car and the twists and turns of the road as they sway from side to side. It's your movie. You have the basic words to work with, but since they mean different things to different people your movie is totally yours. The author may have had one thing in mind, but when it's not fully described some portion is left to your imagination.

Suppose it's important for you to recall the words "Stanford University." If you are familiar with the college then see it, hear the sounds on campus, feel yourself as part of the student body, or perform an action such as playing on a team, or doing an experiment in a science lab. If you are not familiar with this particular school, find an association that you already have in your mind that sounds like or is spelled like Stanford. Do you know a person by the name of Stan that you can visualize? Or think of smaller words that are a part of the whole word, such as *stand* and *Ford*. See yourself standing next to a Ford automobile. As you stand next to it, hear the engine of the Ford. Feel yourself turn the key to start the car. After standing next to the Ford, jump in and drive it away. There are times when these small details may not be important, such as when you're reading for pleasure, but when you are going to be held accountable for what you read, these associations will help you retain the information long after you close the book.

Go on to read the next group of words: "As he stood before Louis Janin . . ." Again, ask yourself, "What am I seeing (hearing or saying, feeling, or experiencing) on my movie screen now?" Continue rolling your movie cameras along. Without any description of the man, it is up to the each reader to imagine what he is like. Visual learners may picture him, auditories may hear him talk, tactiles may feel what kind of personality he has, and kinesthetics may find themselves shaking hands with him. Again, to remember his name, think of a Louis you know in person, a famous personality, or someone from history and visualize him. Janin may not ring a bell with you, so associate it with some similar-looking or -sounding word: Jan, Janie, or Jan "in" a place. Insert the association into your movie as a flashback or cutaway to help you remember the person's name.

Take the next group of words: "one Friday morning . . ." Note that if there are a variety of images, you can sometimes break a sentence into phrases, but sometimes you can work with a whole sentence. The benefit of breaking a sentence up in the beginning stages is that sometimes, when the sentence has too much going on in it, you tend to only visualize a part of it, skipping over some images. Until you get used to this technique, imagine everything. You will discover for yourself how much you can read at a time so you do not miss anything. Back to the "Friday morning." What comes on your movie screen when you think of a Friday morning? The visuals may see a group of people at the office reading the weekend entertainment section of the newspaper to plan their days off. The auditories may hear themselves discussing where they want to go Friday afternoon after work. The tactiles may feel excitement over the upcoming weekend. The kinesthetics may be passing out tickets that they picked up for their friends at the office for a basketball game for the next day.

Next, the passage reads: ". . . he was told there was only a stenographer position available." Go ahead and experience that in your own sensory modality on your movie screen. See a stenographer at work, hear the sound of someone hitting the keys, feel the sensation of your fingers on the keys, or feel your arm movements as you strike the keys.

The story continues: "'I'd love it!' exclaimed the excited young man." Although this is an auditory image and the auditories will hear the words, in their movie the visuals may see the expression on the man's face, the tactiles may feel the excitement of having a chance at the job, and the kinesthetics may experience themselves jumping up, or hitting their fist into the air with a loud "Yes!"

The passage next reads: "'However, I can't start until next Wednesday.'" Ask yourself what you see, hear, say, feel, or do on your movie screen next. Are you visual learners seeing the man pointing to Wednesday on a calendar? Are you auditories hearing yourself say "Wednesday," or associating it with a favorite television show you watch on Wednesdays? Are you tactiles feeling yourself write the word *Wednesday* in your day-timer? Are you kinesthetics remembering Wednesday because that is the day you go to exercise class or do your food shopping?

Read the rest of the passage by yourself, breaking it up as follows between the slashes: "Bright and early on Wednesday morning,/ the young man reported for duty./ 'I like the promptness and enthusiasm,' Janin assured the lad./ 'I do have one question. Why couldn't you start on Monday?'/ 'Well, you see, sir, I had to find a typewriter and learn how to use it,'/ replied, the young man—Herbert Hoover—who would become president of the United States."

As you read each of the above phrases, remember the question to ask yourself that applies to your visual, auditory, tactile, or kinesthetic learning link. Remember, you will have to be thinking the question to yourself as you read without anyone else reminding you. The question is: "What am I seeing (hearing or saying, feeling, or doing) on my movie screen now?" With practice, you will no longer need to ask this question in your mind; you will just automatically convert the words into the movie. Do not skip anything, because you will find that what you did not picture in your mind may be lost even minutes after you read it. What you do picture will be there long after you read the passage.

Now, prove to yourself how much of the passage you remember. Answer the following questions about your "movie." When you reply, give only the basic answer that appeared in the *printed* story and leave out the additional information you created and added to help you remember. Answer purely from memory without looking at the passage again. No peeking back!

1. Whom is this story about?
2. What was he looking for?
3. What school did he go to?
4. What day did he have the interview?
5. What part of the day did he have the interview?
6. Who interviewed him?
7. What position was available?
8. How did he feel about taking the position that was available?
9. What day did he want to start?
10. Why did he choose that day?

ANSWERS: (Note: you may have added the description you made in your mind to the answers, but the basic answers are below:)

1. Possible answers are: a young man, an eager young man, or Herbert Hoover.
2. a part-time job, or a part-time job to help him through school
3. Stanford University
4. Friday
5. morning
6. Louis Janin, or a man
7. stenographer

8. He was excited, or, he said, "I'd love it."
9. Wednesday
10. He needed time to learn how to type.

The key to experiential comprehension is to visualize the passage as vividly as you can using your best learning sense. When you visualize and make it real your brain is taking it in as if it were actually happening to you. We tend to remember events that seem real to us better than we remember those we read about. Think of how real a dream seems. It is not really happening, but while we are experiencing it, it feels real to us. Those who can recall their dreams find that they can remember them as clearly as events in their lives. We can use that same mental ability to help us remember what we read for the purpose of learning. If we experience the passage as if it were really happening to us, we will comprehend it and remember it better. Thus, visual learners will feel as if they really saw it, auditories as if they really heard it, tactiles as if they really felt it, and kinesthetics as if they really did it. It is startling to see how people who were previously scoring anywhere from a D or F on comprehension tests in a wide variety of subjects began to score an A when they used this method. They learned how to achieve total comprehension of whatever they read. Others, marveling at their friend's new "ability," often wanted to learn it too. The beauty of the method is that it can be learned by anyone of any age.

Did you ever wonder how a teenager can study for hours for a test and come home with a low grade, yet can rattle off every sports statistic of his or her favorite team, all the players, and give you a detailed description of each of their games? Does he or she have a comprehension problem? Certainly not, as evidenced by his or her seemingly fantastic comprehension when it comes to sports. It's just that this material—action sports—may be compatible with his or her learning link, while the material he or she is studying is probably not action-oriented. But anything can be converted to a medium he or she will understand. If the material were converted into action in a step-by-step way, then your teen would remember it as vividly as the sports event.

This method can work with *any* reading material, both fiction and nonfiction. The key is to convert anything you read into a video or a movie. Think about how many scientific documentaries you see on television. They even make movies and videos about math, language, history, and computers. When you read in these various content areas all you are doing is becoming the producer or director and making a movie out of the material. You can even do this with abstract subjects that do not even seem to have any action. We will now see how to use experiential reading with a technical passage, provided below. The same technique can be used for reading texts in science, math, social sciences, technology, and content that is not about people or action. Do not read the passage until you follow the directions below the passage called "How to Read the Sample Technical Passage 'Photosynthesis.'"

Sample Technical Passage: "Photosynthesis"

Photosynthesis is a biochemical reaction that occurs when a green plant takes in sunlight, carbon dioxide from the air, and water, and converts them using its chlorophyll into carbohydrates and oxygen.

How to Read the Sample Technical Passage "Photosynthesis"

Start with the first phrase: "Photosynthesis is a biochemical reaction that occurs when a green plant . . ." If you know what photosynthesis is, ask yourself, "How can I represent this on my movie screen so viewers will know what it is? What am I seeing (hearing or saying, feeling, or doing)?" If you do not know what photosynthesis is, the passage cues you by saying, "a biochemical reaction," which lets you know that the rest of the sentence will tell you what it is. If you first need to read the whole sentence to picture photosynthesis, then do so, or look it up in a dictionary. On their movie screen, the visual learners may see a green plant with thick leaves growing in their flower garden. The auditories may hear the sounds in the garden, with the birds chirping in the trees or bees buzzing around the garden. The tactiles may feel themselves sunning themselves next to the plant on a warm summer day, enjoying the gentle breeze blowing. The kinesthetics may experience themselves digging in the garden.

Let's read on: "takes in sunlight." What is happening in your movie now? The visuals may see the sun's rays entering the green plant. The auditories may hear the words or a vibratory sound representing light waves reaching the plant. The tactiles may feel the warm rays penetrate their skin. The kinesthetics may travel from the sun down to the plant.

Next it says: "carbon dioxide from the air." How will you portray carbon dioxide on your movie screen? The visual learners may see the symbol CO_2 or a drawing of a molecule of one carbon atom and two oxygen molecules. Or they may see a person who is exhaling carbon dioxide gas. The auditories may hear "CO_2" or the sound of these molecules bouncing around. Or they may hear someone exhaling carbon dioxide. The tactiles may feel themselves write "CO_2" or feel themselves as a carbon dioxide molecule floating gently in the air and suddenly being squeezed through the plant's soft leaves. The kinesthetics may imagine themselves writing "CO_2," with their arm tracing it in the air or writing on a flip chart, or experience themselves bouncing around in the air, knocking into many other molecules, and then being forcefully sucked into the plant.

The reading continues: "and water." What is on your movie screen now? The visual learners may see water as a blue lake surrounded by a green forest. The auditories may hear the sound of the water in the ocean crashing on the shore. The tactiles may feel themselves floating peacefully in the ocean, enjoying the waves lapping against their skin. The kinesthetics may experience themselves surfing the waves in the ocean. Whatever it takes to remember what you read is fair game.

Next it says: "and converts them using its chlorophyll." Again, you may or may not know what chlorophyll is. If you don't know, what happens to your movie? You cannot make an image for that scene now you have a gap in your movie. The viewers are suddenly lost because the screen went blank. This shows what happens when we skip over vocabulary words we do not know: There is suddenly a gap in our understanding. At this point what you need to do is look the word up. Get a dictionary, or use a glossary in the text and find out, on the spot, what it is. If you wait you may forget to look it up, or when you look it up later it is out of context and will not be as meaningful. If you stop and look up an unknown vocabulary word at the point that it enters the scene in the movie you will remember it because you actively "directed it" in your movie, and then it makes sense in the context. So let's look up "chlorophyll" first so we can proceed with the movie. We look in a glossary and find that chlorophyll is green material in the tissues of plants used for photosynthesis. Now, back to your movie. Visual learners may see little green particles in the leaf of the plant taking in carbon dioxide and water, letting the sun cook them together. The auditories may hear the little green particles vibrating the carbon dioxide and water as it does its conversion process. The tactiles may feel like they *are* the chlorophyll, opening their hands to hold the incoming carbon dioxide and water, and feel the warmth of the sun shaking them, heating them together to convert the substances. The kinesthetics may experience themselves sucking in the carbon dioxide and water, and when the sun bombards them, shaking them at high speed to convert them.

Next, we read: "into carbohydrates." How will you portray carbohydrates in your movie now? The visual learners may see a plate full of carbohydrates. The auditories may hear the sound of someone crunching carbohydrates. The tactiles may feel themselves eating carbohydrates, enjoying their taste and the sensation of their texture in their mouths. The kinesthetics may feel themselves eating some carbohydrates as they rush out to the gym to exercise.

Finally, we conclude the passage by reading: "and oxygen." How will you show that to viewers in the audience? Visual learners may show themselves outdoors, taking a deep breath, and breathing in little oxygen molecules that they see on their screen.

The auditories may hear themselves take that deep breath. The tactiles will feel the oxygen entering their mouths and traveling down their windpipes and into their lungs. The kinesthetics may be running on the track and taking in deep gulps of oxygen, feeling the muscles of their chest expand as they breathe in.

Now let's test your comprehension on this one. Answer without looking back at the passage. As a question comes up, relax and recall the movie you created. Do not try to force yourself to remember the words—just let the images come up. Visuals will relax and say, "What did I see?" Auditories, "What did I hear?" Tactiles, "What did I feel?" Kinesthetics, "What did I do?"

1. What is this passage about?
2. What do green plants do?
3. What is needed for this process to take place?
4. What does chlorophyll do?
5. What two things do green plants give off after chlorophyll converts the ingredients it took in?

ANSWERS:

1. photosynthesis (or a description of photosynthesis)
2. convert sunlight, carbon dioxide, and water into oxygen and carbohydrates
3. chlorophyll (or sunlight, carbon dioxide, and water)
4. convert sunlight, carbon dioxide, and water into oxygen and carbohydrates
5. oxygen and carbohydrates

You can see how this process works well with technical material. Anything can be pictured as a movie, and you will remember it much better because the reading material becomes an activity you experienced through your best learning style.

You may also understand from the above example why we have to read the passage in small parts. Remember, whatever we do not portray in our movie may be forgotten. Technical reading requires more careful attention than pleasure reading. Since there are so many technical details, we need to take the time to picture everything. If we do not, we will take double, triple, or quadruple the time to learn by reading the passage over and over in the hopes that we will remember each detail. But by experiencing it as a movie or as live action, we can recall it with even one careful reading.

You may now say that this feels as if it is taking you longer to read. First of all, this was a demonstration to teach you how to do it, so I was "talking you" through the process. Second, because I addressed four different learning styles it felt longer—but you will only be asking yourself the question related to your learning style. Third, you will be asking the question in your own mind, which is faster. Fourth, after practicing for a few days or weeks you will not need to verbalize the question anymore; you will automatically convert the words into images. Think of it as taking a bite of food, chewing, and swallowing—you take a bite of the word, digest it, and get the image. Fifth, the process of reading a word and getting an image will not be two separate occurrences; they will happen simultaneously. You will reach a point when you read the word and the images appear immediately, and you can clip along at a fast pace, getting a series of images without even being aware of reading words. That is what good readers do.

It is also something *everyone* can learn to do. With practice, you will not even be aware that you are reading, but will instantly be absorbed in the movie you made in your mind as you turn the pages of a book. You may never have learned to read this way and suddenly find how enjoyable it is to have an entire movie playing out in your head as you turn the pages. This is why there are millions of people who enjoy reading— they are getting these experiential movies in their heads. Did you ever hear some people say they prefer reading the book to seeing the movie of the same title? Why? First, because they experience the book as a movie, imagining the scenes based on their own experiences. After all, that is what the film-maker or screenwriter is doing. They have taken the same script you are reading in book form and converted it to images on the screen.

When you read the book yourself you are the director, and you can determine the actors, actresses, and scenery, even putting yourself and people you know into the story and living it as if you are there. That is why it is so engrossing and engaging for some people to read and why they can't put a book down until they're finished. Second, in a book you also experience the feelings and thoughts of the characters, while on a movie screen you can only infer them from the actors' facial expressions, tones of voice, words, or actions. We can relate to the characters, share their experience, and know that others go through many of the same emotions and thoughts that we have. We can also find solutions to our problems as they work through theirs.

EXERCISE: Practice experiential comprehension with your own reading material. For the purpose of the initial exercise, chose a fictional piece with descriptions of a person doing something. Take a paragraph or two and read it in the way we read the two samples above. Ask yourself what is happening in your movie and either describe it in your head or aloud. If you want a partner to help you, have him or her ask you, "What is happening in your movie?" Describe the scenes phrase by phrase, or sentence by sentence. Visual learners will see it, auditories will hear it, tactiles will feel it, and kinesthetics will act out the action. If you are a combination of learning styles, you will combine several senses. After reading the page, ask yourselves questions to recall what you read, or have someone ask questions about the passage for you. If you cannot think of the questions to ask, just relay back everything you remember that happened in your movie, and then check your response against the text to verify how much you recalled.

Eliminating Blocks to Comprehension

There are several blocks to comprehension that hinder us as we read or listen. Many people struggle to read and go through life never learning how to eliminate these blocks. They are: being unable to associate new learning with the knowledge they already have; misunderstanding the terminology and vocabulary; and being unable to break words down into syllables to figure out the longer words. This next section will take each of these factors and show you how to eliminate these problems to help accelerate your learning.

Hooking Information Into Our Prior Knowledge

When we are first faced with information, the brain perceives it either visually, auditorially, tactilely, or kinesthetically, and asks one question: "Do I recognize this information?" It searches its database of memories and comes up with three possible answers:

1. Yes, I already know this information.
2. It is similar to something I know, but different in some ways.
3. No, I do not know this information at all.

The brain proceeds to do some further activities based on which of the above answers it comes up with.

If the brain already knows the information it just reconfirms it; it does not have to put in any further effort to alter its knowledge-base. For example, while shopping in the grocery store we see the cauliflower stand and we recognize "cauliflower." We do not give it much thought because we already know it.

If the brain finds that the information is similar but not exactly like what is in its memory, it will evaluate the ways it is similar and how it differs. It will then link the new information to that specific memory that is similar, making an association with what it knows. The brain cuts down its work of assimilating the new information because it says, "Oh, it is just like that other thing I already have in my memory. I only have to remember what makes it different." It is easier to learn information associated with what we already know because we only need to accommodate the differences. For example, we see green cauliflower in the store. We stop and think, "Oh, this is something new. It looks like cauliflower in shape but like broccoli in color.

You read the sign and it says, "Broccoflower." You now alter your mental database to accommodate a new form of cauliflower that is green like broccoli, or a new form of broccoli that looks like cauliflower, depending upon how you look at it.

If the brain decides that it does not know the information at all, then it has more work to do, slowing down the process. It has to create a new memory connection for the information and learn more about what "it" is. In most cases, the brain will try to avoid this step and stay with the step above—linking it to something it already knows because it is easier. For example, you are in the grocery store and see a vegetable whose shape, color, and name you never saw or heard of before. You have no idea of what it tastes like, how you prepare it, where it comes from, or what it is used for. You have a lot of work to do to find additional data about this vegetable. Chances are if you came across the word for that vegetable in a text you may recall seeing it, but have no idea what it is, and could not easily comprehend that text. It would be a lot easier if someone said to you, "This vegetable is like squash, tastes like squash, but differs in shape and color." Then it would be easier for you to hook it into your memory bank with data on squash.

Thus, the first step in comprehension is to make associations between the new material and the old. When we are learning something new we want to find a way to connect it to our prior knowledge. Think of it as a computer database in which certain programs already exist in the hard drive. If we insert a floppy disk containing a program not on the hard drive, the computer would not be able to recognize and read it. We would have to convert the format of the program on the floppy disk into what is on the hard drive to be able to "comprehend" it.

Understanding New Terminology and Vocabulary

We need to use terminology or vocabulary to understand new data. We may encounter a new object, concept, or idea, but unless we can use terminology or vocabulary that we already know, we will not understand the meaning or function of the new data. It is like learning a word from another language. The word is only a collection of sounds and letters until we know its definition. Only then can we interpret the information and comprehend it.

If we are learning the material on our own and we come across an unfamiliar word, we need to first define it and then try to connect it to something similar in our memory. To define the new information, we may need to look in a reference source such as a dictionary, glossary, or encyclopedia. If it is a term found in a book, then the first time the information appears we need to look back to previous pages, where it will usually be defined. There we can find written examples or graphic illustrations. On a CD-ROM computer program we can use hypertext, in which we click on the word and an elaboration or definition of the word appears. Or, we can ask someone what it means.

We need to take responsibility for finding the definition. Often when we don't know a new term, we just skip over it for one reason or another. This is how we develop faulty comprehension: By not bothering to find out what each new bit of information means, we create a gap in our understanding. Suppose that information turns up again, over and over, in the material. Our comprehension continues to drop because further knowledge is dependent on the terms we skipped over. This could happen when we are reading, listening to a lecture, or doing a procedure. If we do not take the time to understand the meaning of each term, we will fumble because we won't understand the material.

Hopefully, when we are learning from an instructor or from print material, audio-visual material, or computers, the presentation will adequately ensure that new information is properly defined for you. But there is no way for the teacher to guess what you already know from your prior education. Thus, it is up to us as learners to ask for clarification when something is new or unfamiliar, and learn how to look up information in reference materials ourselves.

As you learn, you should keep track of any vocabulary or

terminology you don't understand. If you are visual, tactile, or kinesthetic, write it down as a reminder to look up the definition at the first available opportunity. If you are auditory, stop and ask questions as soon as it is feasible. You can then use your learning link to define the word in the following ways:

Visual Left-Brain: Read the word and its definition. Make a list of the new words so they can be seen or reread.

Visual Right-Brain: Make a diagram or mind map of the word, the definition, and a pictorial clue.

Auditory Left-Brain: Talk about the word and its definition and use it in a sentence.

Auditory Right-Brain: Talk about an association between the sound of the new word with a word you already know. Then make up an imaginative story that connects the old word you know, the new word, and its definition. For example: *cacophony* means "horrible sound or noise." Think: "caco" sounds like *cackle,* a word I already know, which is a sharp, broken noise or cry that hens make, or a laugh imitating a hen. If you did not know that "phon" is derived from the Greek word for *sound*, you could also think of *telephone.* In your imaginary story you may pick up a telephone and hear the horrible cackling of hens on the other end, and connect it to the word's meaning of "horrible sound." Thus, when you hear the word *cacophony* you will think about hens cackling on the phone, and remember it means "horrible noise or sound."

Tactile Left-Brain: Write the word and its definition in a list and write an association for the word connecting it with your feelings or an emotional situation in the past in which the word could be used. Write the new word on a card and the definition on other cards, and use your hands to arrange the cards to match. Play games with new words involving your hands.

Tactile Right-Brain: Write the word and its definition in a colorful, creative way and draw pictures to go with it, or use a mind map. Connect the word to feelings you have about it or some situation in the past involving emotions that relate to the word. Visualize yourself recreating a movie of the circumstance in your mind, using the new word in its associated situation.

Kinesthetic Left-Brain: · Take large paper and, while standing up, write the word and the definition in a list and relate to an action to go with the meaning. Act out the word in a situation in which it would be used. If that is not possible, visualize yourself acting out a situation that involves the word. Do a movement activity as you read through your list of words and their definitions.

Kinesthetic Right-Brain: Take large paper and, while standing up, write the word in large size and in color with the definition arranged as a mind map with action drawings accompanying the meanings. Act out the word in a pantomime that relates to the word. Visualize yourself acting out a situation that would involve the word, or make up an imaginative story using the new word, others you already know that sound similar, and the definition of the new word. Do a physical activity, such as bouncing a ball, jogging in place, or pedaling an exercise bike while reading back your words and their meanings.

You will find that it will be easier to learn the meanings of unfamiliar words and terms when you do so according to your best learning link.

Reading Words Syllable by Syllable

The techniques in this chapter can be used for several purposes. They can eliminate blocks to comprehension due to not knowing how to read all the sounds in English. They can also be applied to learning a different language. Finally, they can be used to learn symbols in various technical languages such as computer languages, science, math, or any other fields that have specialized symbols.

One difficulty that prevents us from understanding the meanings of the words we read, either in English or in another language, is that we may not be able to say a word because we do not know what sounds the letters make. English is a complicated language because one letter may have many sounds. There are a surprising number of adults whom I have met, many with high school and even college degrees, who cannot properly read passages aloud that contain multi-syllabic words or a higher-level vocabulary because they don't know how to read the more complicated letter patterns in those words. Many of them find their comprehension suffers because they end up skipping over the "hard" words. In some languages you only have to learn one sound for each letter, but in English, did you know that there are over twenty-five ways to read and spell the letter *o*, depending upon which letters it is next to? For example, *o* can be pronounced and combined with different letters to give us: *hot*, *rope*, *go*, *toe*, *boat*, *book*, *boot*, *out*, *through*, *bought*, *dough*, *rough*, *could*, *cow*, *row*, *other*, *or*, *tore*, *door*, *soar*, *doll*, *troll*, *hole*, *goal*, *oil*, *boy*. If someone does not learn all the possible combinations for each vowel sound, it is easy to misread words. Thus, many people have reading problems both in English and in other languages, because they have not learned all the sound combinations. How did this happen? There are a startling number of students in upper grades and adults who can't convert the letters they see on the page into their correct sounds because they never mastered the letter-sound relationships. Often adults notice this problem for the first time only when they are given technical reading material, professional journals, or training materials to read at the workplace, and they suddenly realize they do not have all the tools to tackle the task. They considered themselves readers, and often didn't notice the problem because many popular books, magazines, and newspapers are written for a lower reading level. These adults may have previously figured out words only from their contexts. Sometimes they may have been accurate and at other times they may have been far from guessing the actual word. As a result, they either read the wrong word and didn't comprehend the reading material, or they skipped the word and were left with a gap in their comprehension.

Some people can comprehend what they read when they know all the words, but when they can't read the words correctly, it seems that they have a comprehension problem. In fact, they do not have a comprehension problem; they have a letter-sound relationship problem. Someone may try to help them by giving endless comprehension exercises to boost their abilities in that area, but their problem is a different one—they need to learn how to read the words before they can answer questions based on what they actually read—not what they guessed they read.

If you find that you struggle with hard words, it may be because you don't know the correct pronunciation of some patterns. If you don't have this difficulty, you can still apply the following section to learning the letter-sound relationships of another language. If you have to learn a second language, you will accelerate your learning by using your best learning link. To accelerate reading instruction, all the letter-sound relationships should be taught in the first year or two, along with comprehension, vocabulary, and independent reading strategies. If, instead of just learning a few of the sounds in the first year of reading, students of all ages, including adults, learned all the sounds in that first year, they would accelerate their reading abilities as well as their speed.

The following are techniques to learn the letter-sound relationships through each learning link:

Visual Left-Brain Learner: Look at the letter printed on a page, a chalkboard, or in a book, accompanied by a picture clue and an example word that begins with that letter. Play games that involve matching the letters and patterns. Do word searches with the letters and patterns. Play step-by-step word games and arrange letter tiles to form words.

Visual Right-Brain Learner: Look at the letter printed in a book, on a chart or poster, or on a chalkboard, in color with a nice design, along with a picture clue and example word. Notice the shape and patterns of the letter. Play games that involve matching the shapes of the letters or the patterns. Do word searches with the letters and patterns. Play imaginative word games with the letter tiles. Create your own words with the letters.

Auditory Left-Brain Learner: Look at the letter and say it aloud, then look at and say words that start with the letter. Verbalize any rules for remembering the letter. Talk about the strokes needed to make the letter, such as *b* is a "stick" followed by a "ball." Talk about the words in sentences. Narrate stories using the words in the sentences. Play oral word games in which you use the words.

Auditory Right-Brain Learner: Look at the letter and say it aloud in a rhythmic way. Look at and say any words that go with the letter in a rhythmic or rhyming way. Put it to music. Recite or sing a little jingle or make a rap to help you recall the sound. Another technique is to tell imaginative stories using words with the letter-sound pattern. Play auditory word games with the patterns.

Tactile Left-Brain Learner: Write the letter on paper or on a chalkboard, or write it in some other way; for example, in sand with your finger. Write any sample words to go with it and draw a picture clue that starts with that letter. Make words with the letter using letter cards. Write rules for pronouncing the letter. Type the words on a computer. Find words for things or people you like that start with the letter. Write sentences connecting the words to your feelings.

Tactile Right-Brain Learner: Write the letter on paper or on a chart in bright colors in a decorative way. Draw a picture clue to go with it and write the word for the picture. Make an arts and crafts picture of the letter. Outline the shape with different colored markers or crayons. Type the words on a computer. Find words for things or people you like that begin with the letter; draw the people or things and write words to name or describe them. Write imaginative stories using the words.

Kinesthetic Left-Brain Learner: Write the letter in the air in large print with the arm muscles of your writing hand, or write the letter on the wall with the light of a flashlight using all your arm muscles (techniques of Barbara Meister Vitale, author of *Unicorns are Real: A Right-Brained Approach to Learning*). Stand up and write the letter in large print on a flip chart, chalkboard, or dry-erase board. Use large three-dimensional letter blocks and move them around to make words. Draw the letters in chalk on the sidewalk about six feet tall, and walk along the letters, saying them as you go. Learn any rules for pronouncing the letters. Play step-by-step games to learn the patterns.

Kinesthetic Right-Brain Learner: Write the letter in the air with the arm you use for writing, or write it on the ceiling with a flashlight. Write the letter large while standing up at a flip chart and draw an action picture that starts with the letter. Use large three-dimensional letter blocks and move them around to make words. Walk along the letter drawn on the sidewalk while saying it and seeing it. Make the letter with your body while saying it and seeing it. Do an action that starts with the letter and say and see the letter as you do the action. As you say the letter and words that start with it, throw a basketball into a net, bounce a ball, or do some activity with your body. Hang up your letters and words where you can see them, and read the letter and matching words while doing an activity or your favorite hobby, such as sitting on an exercise bike, walking around the room, hitting a golf ball, jumping rope, or throwing a basketball. Give yourself points for each time you read the word and make a basket. Reward yourself for a certain number of points. Play games to learn the patterns.

For more activities for each learning style refer to my previous book, *Solving Your Child's Reading Problems*, (New York: Citadel Press, 1995) and *Unicorns Are Real: A Right-Brained Approach to Learning*, by Barbara Meister Vitale (California: Jalmar Press, 1982).

When you learn the letter-sound relationship either in English or another language, through your correct learning style, learning is accelerated, easier, and more fun because you are working in your element.

What About Listening Comprehension?

The examples in this chapter have described comprehension tasks as related to reading, but listening comprehension involves the same skills. The same strategies for using our best learning link described in the above sections on comprehending what we read can be used to comprehend what we hear when listening to a speaker, either in person, on audiotape or videotape, in the movies, or on CD-ROM.

22

How to Improve Your Memory

Did you know that you could improve your memory by using your superlink? A good memory is not something that some people are born with and others without. Memory can be developed. The only difference between someone with a good memory and someone with a poor one is training. This chapter provides a practical, easy-to-use guide to improving your memory using your superlink to accelerate your learning.

Training Your Memory

We have a tremendous amount of data stored in our brains that we can pull up at will. One reason we do not remember certain things is that we didn't make an effort to remember them for an extended period of time. Consciously or unconsciously, we *chose* to remember those items we do remember. If we want to improve our memory, we can do so by training ourselves to remember what we want when we want.

When we talk of learning anything quickly, we want to learn the subject as well as recall it for more than just a moment. Sadly, when many schools teach a subject, the students know it only until they are tested on it. Give them a surprise test a month or two later and all that hard work to learn the subject seems to have been for naught. How is it possible that we can spend six months to a year taking a course and forget what we learned years later? It is not that we do not have a good memory—we just don't have a *trained* memory. Accelerated learning involves training our memory using our superlink.

Long-Term and Short-Term Memory

We have two memory systems: short-term and long-term.

Short-term memory holds something temporarily in your mind until you decide what to do with it. Consciously or unconsciously, you can either decide to store it in your long-term memory or dismiss it as something unimportant. Our short-term memory is a revolving door with new information entering continually. It can be compared to a computer screen memory. Information stays there as long as you are focusing on it and working with it. Then you must decide whether to save it in the hard drive or on a disk—the computer's long-term memory—or let it be erased when you turn the computer off.

Long-term memory permanently holds something in your memory. There are many things we learned in childhood that were placed in our long-term memory that we have not forgotten: walking, riding a bicycle, speaking your language, writing the alphabet, childhood songs and nursery rhymes, among other things. These memories become a part of our database from which we can draw at any time.

Keys to Improving Your Memory

The basics of having a good memory are simple and can be learned by people of any age, including young children.

Step 1: Have a purpose or goal for remembering what you are learning.

Step 2: Consciously decide to put what you learn into long-term memory.

Step 3: Use your superlink to store what you learn in your long-term memory.

Step 4: Keep a memory active by retrieving it and using it.

Step 1: Have a Purpose or Goal for Remembering What You Are Learning.

We are bombarded with millions of bits of information daily. With the opening of the information superhighway we have access to a huge amount of information circulating in the world on a daily basis. If we were to recall every single sensory impression and bit of information we receive we would be so overwhelmed that we would not be able to focus on the range of activities that were more important to our lives. Life is too short to learn everything about everything; we must make a conscious choice about what we want to remember. This process involves deciding why we need to learn something. When we want to learn something, we must also decide why it is important for us to learn it. If we keep that goal in mind we will put our brain on notice that this is material we *want* to remember.

Why did you remember your name as a child? When you figured out that people kept asking you your name, you decided that the next time they asked you had better know it. Why did you learn those twenty-six meaningless sounds called the alphabet when you were just a toddler? You had no idea what they stood for or what words they went with, but you learned how to repeat those twenty-six sounds that might well have been nonsense to you. Why did you learn it? Maybe you figured out that your parents would show you off to their friends by having you repeat the alphabet and would give you that big smile and hug that you loved. Or maybe you surmised that your relatives would give you a quarter for being such a "good and smart" child for saying your ABC's. You had a purpose for learning that information at age two, three, or four that had nothing to do with getting a high school diploma. You could have just as easily been taught the ABC's in a foreign language, or the periodic table of the elements, or the names of all the bones of the body. We learned what we did because someone valued it, rewarded us for knowing it with either verbal or nonverbal gestures or material gifts, and this made us feel good.

The same principle holds true today when it comes to learning. You really wanted to learn how to drive so you mastered the physical act of driving along with the driver's manual and all of its facts, figures, and state laws. The same people who can't pass a social studies test can pass a written driving examination on technical information and legal terms. Why? They wanted to remember the driver's education manual because it meant they could have wheels. It is the same brain reading that manual that reads other textbooks. Is there a selective gene in our body that discriminates between learning a driver's education manual and a political science course? Not at all. It is our intention and desire to learn something that determines what we will remember and what we will forget.

Some possible reasons, purposes, or goals for learning are: to advance in our career; to improve our skills; to raise our salary; to get a promotion; to become certified in a field; to pass a test; to keep up with new knowledge; to help others; for enjoyment, personal growth, curiosity, or many other reasons.

EXERCISE: Take the subject you chose to study as you worked through the book and write a sentence or two stating why you want to learn more about this subject.

Step 2: Consciously Decide to Put What You Learn Into Long-Term Memory.

We must program our minds to send information into our long-term memory if we wish to retain it. Otherwise we will get the information, comprehend it, but it will be erased shortly afterwards. If we want to recall it for the long haul, we have to establish the reason for wanting to put it into long-term memory and the length of time we want it to stay in memory. Many people find they can't remember what they read, hear, or study long enough to pass a test. This is because they don't program themselves to recall everything they learn for the entire duration of the course of study.

Here are some things to think about when you're trying to commit what you learn to long-term memory:

1. If you learn it the first time you read or hear it you won't have to go over the material again and again, wasting precious time.
2. You can work towards your promotion, advancement, or passing a test or course faster.
3. You will have more free time to do other things.
4. You will be able to use the information right away.

Decide that you want to commit what you learn to your long-term memory, the length of time you want to retain it, and why it is important for you to learn it.

EXERCISE: Using the subject you selected to learn as you work through this book, write your reasons for putting what you learn about the subject into long-term memory.

Step 3: Use Your Superlink to Store What You Learn in Your Long-Term Memory.

This is the key to the entire process. I developed this technique as an extension of the application of learning links. It works so incredibly quickly that everyone who has used it is amazed at how sharp one's memory becomes.

The secret is: The key to remembering what we learned is to store it according to our best learning link.

If we are visual people, we have an excellent memory for visual detail. If we are auditory, we have a sharp memory when it comes to auditory detail. If we are tactile, we remember best what we feel, either physically or emotionally. Those who are kinesthetic remember best what they did and how their body moved.

Do you remember your experiential comprehension? As you read or listened you converted the information into an experience in your mind that matched your learning link.

Visual people would *see* what they read and heard as a movie in their minds.

Auditory people would *hear* what they read and heard as the sound track to a movie in their minds, complete with words, music, or sound effects.

Tactile people would *experience or feel* the sensations and feelings of the movie in their minds.

Kinesthetic people would *act out* the events of the movie in their minds.

By experiencing what you read or hear using your superlink, you are tricking your mind into thinking an event is really happening to you. You have involved yourself in a true virtual reality experience that is taking place inside your mind through your best sense, supported by the other senses.

Books or lectures are real events that have been converted into words for the benefit of those who were not there. Writing is like creating a cyberworld in which reality is encoded into words, and reading decodes or converts it back into experiences and events. Reading is like cracking a code so we can recreate the writer's or speaker's experience in our minds. The more vividly we do this and the more we involve ourselves in the action, the more we will experience being there and the more thoroughly we will remember it.

Review Chapter 21 on comprehension, in which you learned how to use the experiential comprehension to match your learning link. This method will increase your memory of what you read. You can review the sample passages or select one of your own. As you read, make a commitment to put this information into long-term memory. Attempt to remember *all* the details of this passage, including names, dates, and other factual details. Read it according to your learning style. For this practice, we will bypass your specialization of having a preference for the right or left side of the brain so you can learn to read using both sides: to remember the big picture and the concrete images (right-side functions), as well as every detail and the words for the experience (left-side functions). Thus, you are going to engage both sides of the brain in the process of reading the passage you select. Convert it into a movie in your mind, either seeing it, hearing it, feeling it, or doing the actions involved. Make associations for words, numbers, and dates with similar words or images already in your mind.

After reading the passage, cover it up and see how much of it you remember now that you've experienced it as an actual event. If you imagined the story in your best learning style you should have found that you can answer every question and recall every detail after picturing a strong image in your mind. If you missed any questions or details, analyze why. Most likely you did not make a strong enough image in your mind or you skipped over part of the text without imagining it. It is always fascinating to see that the text someone doesn't picture is gone from his or her memory when he or she tries to answer the questions, while the material that person did imagine pops out as if he or she really experienced the event.

You can do this kind of reading with everything you read, fiction or nonfiction. You can do this with the daily newspaper, magazine articles, trade journals, memos, bulletins, interoffice communications, E-mail, or faxes. The same technique can work with a novel as well as with scientific material, technical reading, history, social sciences, health, or textbooks on any subjects, medical books, training manuals for any field, or anything else you can think of. You can also use it for listening to lectures. Auditory left-brain people can mentally record material directly, while those with other superlinks can take dictation so they can convert the material into an experiential event at their own pace later.

Anyone can train themselves to read or listen to any material and put it into long-term memory. What does it take? All you have to do is be mentally present as you read. The moment you just look at the words without converting them you have actually stopped reading. Reading only takes place when the words become images or experiences in your mind. Unless you are an auditory left-brain person who gets meaning directly from words without making corresponding images, just reading (for other learning styles) "word, word, word, word" continually without images is not only not reading, it is a boring, useless task that doesn't help you at all. Begin to monitor your reading by making sure you are picturing everything. Remember, the moment you stop visualizing, you have stopped reading. You have begun to daydream. Every word you may have looked at or even said aloud while your mind wandered is gone from your memory because you were not really mentally present. You will then need to return to the last set of words that you pictured and reread that section or it will be lost.

If you are reading in order to learn, you will soon realize that when you do not picture the text as you read you are wasting precious time. Not only do you not comprehend the information, you will not be sending it into long-term memory. This is why you may have had to read the material over and over in the past. But if you are in a hurry and want to learn anything quickly, you need to read it correctly the first time around. You will find that with a little practice you can have total recall of everything you read. Just be attentive, do the conversion process in your best learning style, and with hardly any effort the whole passage will come back to you hours, days, or even weeks later because you transformed it into an experience that happened to you. This method of reading is one of the most powerful tools you will have to speed up your reading and learning.

As you answered the comprehension questions for the sample passage "Rapid Learning" in chapter 21, you may have noticed that as certain key words came up, an image arose in your mind. If you are not auditory and you tried to remember the words, you may have drawn a blank. But if you instead said to yourself, "What did I experience in my movie?" while you were in a relaxed mental state, the movie would have rerun in your head and the answer would have appeared. You were using both your right and left hemisphere of the brain in this process. The image appears in the right side of the brain, and the word for it is recalled from your speech and language centers in the left side (that is, in most people—some people have some language in the right side of the brain). Thus, you have engaged your whole brain in this process. This kind of reading is a great exercise for developing your whole brain. You are making more connections between the two halves of the brain and developing your thinking powers as well.

EXERCISE: Find something to read on the subject you've chosen to learn. Take two or three paragraphs and practice reading them as shown in the sample passage in chapter 21 called "Rapid Learning." After each phrase, ask yourself what you are seeing (if you are visual), hearing (if you are auditory), feeling (if you are tactile), or doing or experiencing (if you are kinesthetic). Read the entire passage in that way and then put the book down and see how many details you can recall, focusing on names, dates, places, and even small facts. Practice reading this way with all reading material from now on until you find you can make the images automatically, the moment you scan the words.

Step 4: Keeping a Memory Active by Retrieving It and Using It.

The next step is to make sure the information stays in your mind as an active file, readily accessible at your fingertips, by deciding how often you need to use the information you learned and for what purposes. Think of it as having material immediately accessible on your computer's hard disk as opposed to putting it on floppy disks and filing them somewhere deep in your closet.

There may be certain types of information that are only needed for a one-time purpose. You may need to pass a test and never need that information again. Suppose you took an art history course that was required for your fine arts degree. You do not want to go into art history, but you do want to be an artist. You need the information to pass the test for your degree, but you do not want to load your mind with dates of famous paintings. Thus, you consciously decide to retain that data only so long as you need it to pass the examination and then let it go. You no longer want to work at keeping that memory active. So you do not devote any more attention to it, and you don't use it or retrieve it anymore. Thus, it is buried by newer, more relevant data that you need to learn.

Step four in training your memory involves making a conscious choice about which long-term memories you wish to keep in an active file and which ones you will allow to be buried in an inactive state. To keep a file active we need to use it and retrieve it periodically. You may not use the dates of the paintings ever again in your life so you let them go, but if you worked as a tour guide in an art museum you would use that information again and again. It would become a part of you and you could instantly bring it from memory, whenever you needed it. If we took a computer course and needed to use what we learned on our jobs every day, we would not want to forget the information after the final examination. By using the information daily, we strengthen the neural network or the interconnections that enable us to perform those functions. Retrieval becomes quicker and more automatic, for when we repeatedly use the information we made a conscious effort to learn; it becomes part of our long-term memory.

Step four requires you to: decide how long you want to keep

what you learned as an active long-term memory, and when and how often you will need to use what you learned; and to make a plan for retrieving and using it regularly. If you decide you need to use it for the one year in which you will be working at a particular job, then you need to spend time practicing using it, doing something with it, or retrieving it daily, weekly, or several times a week so it is fresh in your mind. Put it on your "to-do" list. If you are visual, scan the material or some notes you have. If you are auditory, talk about it to others or yourself. If you are tactile, write it or make something with your hands related to the material. If you are kinesthetic, do something with it. This will keep the memory active. The more you use it, the more automatic retrieving this memory will become.

EXERCISE: Using the subject you're learning as an example, decide: how long you want to retain the information as an active long-term memory; when and how often you will need to use what you learned; and your personal plan for retrieving and using the material regularly.

What About Memorization?

Another kind of memory task is memorization, which involves recalling lists of facts and data. If you find you have to memorize information just to pass a test, then you can also use your learning link to accomplish this task quickly.

I have developed eight different memorization techniques, one for each of the eight superlinks. Try it with a list of data you need to remember. Practice the technique until it becomes automatic.

Take the data you're trying to learn and make associations with something you already know. It can be a word that sounds like or is spelled like the word you need to remember. It can be a person or thing that comes to mind when you think of that word. You need to make up a movie or story in your mind connecting the new word on the list with the old word. The story should be vivid, humorous, imaginative, or far-out—something that will catch your attention and stay in your mind.

The main difference between the left-brain and right-brain technique is that the left-brain people will need to remember the list in order. The right-brain people can make the associations without going in order unless this is required for a test or task; then the right-brain people can use the left-brain technique.

Memorizing Data

Suppose you need to recall the following list of words: *cat, house, moon, apple, football*. Here is how each learning link can do it:

Right Brain: Remember the associations without putting them in order.

Left Brain: Remember them in linear order. Here is one way to do it: Take your hands and lay them palms down in front of you. Using your left hand first, count on your fingers, beginning with the pinkie, as follows: pinkie finger is one, ring finger is two, middle finger is three, pointer or index finger is four, and thumb is five. Now you will imagine that you are attaching each of the five words to each of your five fingers, in order, beginning with the word *cat*. You will do it according to one of the following learning style techniques below:

Visual Technique: You will need to *see* the images and their associations. Here are examples to get you started, but you should make up your own (you will remember the ones you create yourself much better than those given to you by someone else): 1. Connect the cat to your pinkie finger. Make up a story that you can see. Can you see a brown cat licking your pinkie finger? What does the cat look like? 2. Connect the house to your ring finger. Are you getting married and standing in front of the doorway of your house, having your spouse put the ring on your finger? See that as vividly as you can. 3. Connect the moon to your middle finger. Can you see yourself balancing the moon on your middle finger, holding it up high? 4. Now link the pointer, or index finger, to the apple. Can you see yourself drawing an apple with a crayon on the tip of your index finger? See the color and shape vividly. 5. Now link the football to your thumb. See the football hitting your thumb as you try to catch it. Can you see the football bouncing off your thumb and going over the goalpost? See the events happening vividly. Now, when you look back at your five fingers, what do you see? Do you remember all the words?

Auditory Technique: You need to hear associations by talking about them, or making up some device that plays with the sounds of the words. Here are some examples, but you should create your own that are meaningful to you: 1. Hear the cat meowing as it licks your pinkie finger. 2. You are listening to music in your house as you take off the ring from your ring finger, toss it on the ground, and hear the jangle of the gold on the floor. 3. You are an astronaut in a space ship and you use your middle finger to push a button to aim your ship for the moon. Hear the ship's engines boom as you take off. 4. You use your index finger to aim an arrow at an apple, and as you pull back the arrow and let it go, you hear the whiz of it cutting through the air. 5. You hear the shouts from people in the stadium as you grab the football with your thumb, throw it, and hear it whip through the air to the goalpost.

Another auditory method is to work with the sound of the words as follows: 1. name the cat on your pinkie finger Pinkie. 2. Ring the bell of your house. 3. Middle finger starts with *m*, and *moon* starts with *m*. 4. Apple and pointer finger both have *p* in them. 5. A baby says "fumb," which reminds you of fumbling the football. Now, when you name each of your five fingers what do you hear? Do you remember all the words?

Tactile Technique: You are going to feel the sensation and emotions of the associations between the new words and the fin-

gers of your hand: 1. Remember a cat you liked (or did not like?).
Bring it to your memory. Recall your feelings about that cat. Feel
the cat licking your pinkie finger. Stroke the cat's soft fur with
your pinkie finger. How does it feel? 2. Recall your favorite
house. Now imagine yourself putting a ring on the ring finger of
someone you love while in your favorite house. How do you feel?
3. Feel yourself pushing a moon rock with your middle finger.
How does the rock feel to you? What is its texture? Is it hard or
soft? How does it feel? 4. Remember a favorite type of apple
you like to eat. You are mixing applesauce with your pointer finger. How does it feel? Take some with your pointer finger and
lick it. How does the texture feel on your tongue? Do you like
it? 5. You are gripping the football with your thumb as you play.
Feel the ground below your feet as you run towards the goal.
Feel the texture of the football. Do you enjoy playing? Now,
when you touch each of your five fingers what do you feel? Do
you remember all the words?

  Kinesthetic Technique: You will need to act out the
words: 1. You are a cat and are crawling around on the floor.
Take hold of your owner's pinkie finger and drag him or her
on the floor to romp with you. 2. You are building a house and
in your exercise room you hang ropes with large rings to swing
from. Experience yourself swinging from the rings that are
shaped like the ring on your ring finger. 3. You are doing
a handstand on the moon, balancing on your middle finger.
4. You are twirling an apple on your pointer finger and tossing
it up and down in the air. 5. You catch a football with your
thumb and then run to the goal line to make a touchdown.
Now, when you flick each of your five fingers what else are you
doing? Do you remember all the words?

Mnemonics as a Memory Device
for Each Learning Link

You can try another technique, mnemonics, by using the first letter of each word to make either a new word or a sentence using

words that begin with the same first letters as the words in the list. The left-brain people will put the letters in order, while the right-brain people can mix up the order to create other sentences or words.

The **visual people** will see the words on paper or a chart or visualize the words in their minds.

The **auditory people** will hear and say the words or experience themselves saying the words in their minds.

The **tactile people** will write the words or imagine themselves feeling what the words describe.

The **kinesthetic people** will write the words in large print while standing up at a chalkboard, or will use big blocks or cut out shapes with the letters on them and move them around. Or they will experience themselves performing an action with the words in their minds.

For example, to remember the five words *cat*, *house*, *moon*, *apple*, and *football*, here are a left-brain and a right-brain technique:

Left-brain people can put the words in order to make the nonsense word *chmaf: c* for *cat*; *h* for *house*; *m* for *moon*; *a* for *apple*; and *f* for *football*. Or they can make a sentence from the first letter of each word: *Can he make a fire?* Added to that can be the actual words as part of the story. Can he make a fire? Have the moon shining over the house, as the cat, sitting on a football, chews an apple by the fire.

Right-brain people can mix up the order in any way. Since the right side sees all the letters of a word simultaneously and does not put things in sequential order, it can remember them as effectively in any order it likes. For example: "cham(p)." Replace *f* with *p* and associate the *f* with the word *football*: He was the champ in football.

Another technique is to make a sentence with the first letters of each word arranged in any order: *My friend has a cat.* You can then add the relevant words to this sentence to make a story: While you were sitting in your house, under a full moon, your friend came over with the cat, which was playing with a football and an apple.

The key is to make associations that are meaningful to you, that are out of the ordinary, and that tie the new words to the old words in some way.

Memorizing by Creating a Story

Another technique is to connect all the words to make a unified story in which you play an active part. You will either see the story, hear the story, feel the story, or act out the story in your mind. The following is an example: "You and your cat were taken from the house and sent up to the moon. You had apples to eat on the way. When you got to the moon you played football together and it was fun because you could bounce really high."

Memorizing Vocabulary Words in English or Other Languages

Learning any field often requires understanding new terminology and vocabulary, so this section will be useful in many situations. You can use this technique to learn the meaning of new words, either in English or other languages. Remember, the visual learners will make a visual image; the auditories will hear and say the words of the association; the tactiles will feel it; and the kinesthetics will do some action with the words.

English Vocabulary Words:
abase: to lower, humiliate
abashed: embarrassed, ashamed

Step 1: Take the first word and find another one that looks or sounds like it and is already in your memory bank. Example: abase: sounds like *base*, something that is on the ground.
Step 2: Make up a story connecting the word you already

know with the meaning of the new word: I was so humiliated I wanted to sink into the *base*, or the ground.

Step 3: Connect the story with your learning link. Visual learners will see themselves with humiliated looks on their faces, sinking down to the base, or floor. Auditories will hear themselves saying they are humiliated and hear the crash as they fall to the floor. Tactiles will feel themselves being humiliated and feel themselves touch the floor. Kinesthetics will be playing a basketball game and when they lose they are humiliated and will fall down on the base, or floor.

When you see or hear the word *abase* in the story you created, the word will be replayed and the concept of humiliation and lowering will come up as an image, giving you its meaning.

Let's try the next word: abashed: ashamed. The word *abashed* sounds and looks like *bashed*. When you bashed into the wall because you weren't looking, you were ashamed. See it, hear it, feel it, or do it based on your learning style, and the word is yours.

Words in other languages: The same principle can be used to learn words in different languages. For example: Here are steps if you want to remember the French word *maison*, which means "house."

Step 1: Think of a word that sounds like, looks like, or is similar to *maison*, or the parts of the word: May's son; my son; maize or corn; May sun.

Step 2: Make up a story connecting the association with the meaning of the word. Let's take "May sun." Link the hot sun in the sky with your house. You might come up with a sentence such as, "The May sunshine was beating down on my house."

Step 3: Connect the story with your learning style. Visual learners will see it, auditories hear it, tactiles feel it, and kinesthetics will act it out.

Let's try an example with the Spanish word *blanco,* which means "white." Connect *blanco* to a blank sheet of paper which is white. Now you have *blanco* as "white."

A Trained Memory Accelerates Learning

By improving your memory you can learn something correctly the first time and cut down the wasted study time rereading and restudying the same material. You can accelerate your learning by training your memory using your superlink.

23

Note-Taking, Study Skills, and Test-Taking Skills

If this were a perfect world, many people would do away with tests and studying. The word *test* can instill fear in even the most fearless of people. Because people have experienced many painful repercussions from failing a test, taking these has become a dreaded task for many. The only people who seem to actually enjoy tests are those who consistently do well in them and feel a sense of achievement and accomplishment.

Let's analyze what a test is. A child learns how to walk and "tests" his or her ability by taking a few steps. We learn a golf swing, and "test" our ability by practicing. A test is a checkpoint to measure our performance or knowledge. We do this all the time in everyday life. It is not meant to be a system for penalizing us, but a way to gauge or measure what we have mastered and what knowledge or skills we have not yet mastered and may need to relearn or review.

If you are learning something on your own, you should build in checkpoints along the way to insure that you have mastered each section. Breaking a large amount of material into smaller bits can help you manage the subject better. There are three study aids that can help us manage the subject we are learning. They are: note-taking, study skills, and test-taking skills.

There are two applications for these skills. We traditionally associate note-taking, study skills, and test-taking skills with learning from books in traditional classroom settings, seminars, and workshops. This chapter will help you learn better in those situations. The second application is for performance tasks such as learning a skill, job, hobby, sport, dance, craft, an instrument or how to use a computer or another technical instrument. While there may not be any tests we need to prepare for, note-taking, study skills, and test-taking skills can still be useful checkpoints. We may wish to take notes as we learn a performance task, review those notes when we do not have access to our teacher or trainer, and test ourselves by measuring our performance. Thus, as you read this chapter you can apply the information to course work or self-study, textbook or lecture-based courses, and performance tasks.

Note-taking is a way to record what we are learning to shorten our review time. It provides us with a study guide so we do not have to reread material or listen to a lecture again.

Study skills are the techniques we use to make sure we have understood and remember the material we are learning.

Test-taking skills are strategies that prepare us for taking a test.

In this chapter we will learn how to use our superlink for note-taking, study skills, and test-taking skills.

Note-Taking Skills

In the previous chapter we discovered how to put what we have learned into long-term memory. We also learned about the importance of repeatedly retrieving and using the information to keep it easily accessible. One aid to help us in doing this is a set of notes that serve as a simple study sheet to review what we have already learned. The notes trigger our memory and allow us to keep what we learned fresh in our mind. It saves us from flipping through numerous pages of a book or hours of audiotapes to trigger our memories. Instead of going through a fifty-page chapter we can look through several pages of notes to remind us of what we learned.

When taking notes, we do not want to write every word we read and hear. That would be taking dictation. Note-taking is *not* taking dictation; rather, it means writing key phrases to trigger our memory later on. Note-taking goes hand in hand with experiential comprehension and memory techniques; it is not supposed to take their place.

If you read in the experiential comprehension mode that matches your superlink and then use the memory techniques that you learned in the last chapter, you already have the material in memory. Note-taking allows you to jot down some key points to organize what you remember in smaller units. In this way, when you review or study you can group together your memories of one unit or section of a subject and go over those memories together. Think of it as a way to organize the data in your computer into files or records. It is hard to manage a one-thousand-page document, so you break it up into smaller chapters and put them into separate files. Note-taking helps us do that. Then, when we look at the key words we wrote, it brings back our memory of all the material in that unit.

There are note-taking skills to match each learning link. In this chapter you will find out how to take notes to match your learning link.

Two Classifications of Note-Taking—
Left-Brain and Right-Brain

Since left-brain people prefer to work in a linear, sequential way and right-brain people prefer to see all the material at once, we have two basic techniques for taking notes. These methods are adapted further, based on the learning styles of visual, auditory, tactile, and kinesthetic learners, which will give you eight different techniques. First, we will look at the differences between the left-brain and right-brain note-taking techniques.

Left-Brain Note-Taking

Left-brain note-taking needs to be in linear and sequential order. The outline format, listing points in numerical, alphabetical, or chronological order, fits the natural way that left-brain people think. There are two basic techniques that use linear order that are helpful for left-brain people.

Technique 1: Left-Brain Outlining

Since traditional schools followed mostly left-brain techniques, the outline was the method of choice used by most instructors. That was back in the days when everything was taught in a left-brain manner. We are more enlightened today—right? The people who did well in the outline technique of taking notes happened to be the left-brain students. It was the right-brain students who struggled with outlining because they do not think in a linear way.

Outlining involves listing each key point followed by the details that elaborate on that point. Those details may have further elaboration in the form of examples. One example of an outline looks like this:

Title

  I. Key point
      A. Detail
          1. Example
          2. Example
      B. Detail
          1. Example
          2. Example
      C. Detail
 II. Key point
      A. Detail
      B. Detail
      C. Detail
          1. Example
          2. Example

To take notes, you would read a paragraph using your experiential comprehension and memory techniques to match your learning style. After you have totally understood the passage, recall the main idea and its details. Then, reflect on what the main idea and the details are, and insert them into your outline format as shown above. You should write the key point and key words for each detail from memory so you can internalize what you read. If you involve your thinking process by picking out the most important ideas and then the details and examples to support them, it reinforces your memory. We do not want to mindlessly copy the text as our notes. Copying like a parrot can be done without thinking—and without remembering the material.

First we want to comprehend and remember, without notes, what we did. Then we want to convert what we have already remembered into notes, giving conscious thought to what we are doing. This actively involves us in the note-taking process so that we know exactly how the notes are associated with our memory. Then, when we look back at the notes to review for a test a week or two later, the abbreviated notes will trigger the entire memory of that section.

Three Types of Rocks

Below is a sample passage that will be used to illustrate the different note-taking techniques for both left-brain and right-brain people. First you will see what this passage would look like in the left-brain outlining technique, writing the key words in an outline form.

There are three types of rocks: sedimentary, igneous, and metamorphic rocks. These rocks can be found in various places around the world.

Sedimentary rocks are formed by sand, soil, and bits of broken rock settling on one another to form layers. They are compressed together by the pressure of the layers on top of them. Examples of sedimentary rock are sandstone and limestone.

Igneous rocks are formed by the earth's molten magma cooling and hardening to form rock. Examples of igneous rock are obsidian and granite.

Metamorphic rocks are sedimentary and igneous rocks that are melted by the earth's heat and then cooled and hardened to form a new combination. Examples of metamorphic rocks are marble and gneiss.

Title: Three Types of Rocks

I. Three types of rocks: sedimentary, metamorphic, and igneous
II. Sedimentary
   A. Sand, soil, broken rocks settling to form layers
   B. Compressed from the pressure of layers above them
   C. Examples:
      1. Sandstone
      2. Limestone
III. Igneous
   A. Formed by molten magma
   B. Rocks formed by cooling and hardening
   C. Examples:
      1. Obsidian
      2. Granite
IV. Metamorphic
   A. From sedimentary with igneous melting by earth's heat
   B. New rocks formed by cooling and hardening
   C.   Examples:
      1. Marble
      2. Gneiss

Technique 2: Left-Brain Two-Column Note-Taking

Another method that works for left-brain people is left-brain two-column note-taking. In this method, a sheet of paper is divided into two columns. The right side will be used for taking notes in a linear form as you read each paragraph. The left side is used for formulating a question which is answered by the notes on the right side. You begin by reading a paragraph using experiential comprehension and memory using your learning link. After reading the paragraph, decide what is important and write down notes using key words as if in a list. Then look over the list. Decide what topic your notes refer to and formulate a question on that topic. Thus, when you are finished you will have a series of questions in the left-hand column answered by the corresponding notes in the right-hand column.

Step 1: First take notes in the right-hand column. Using the sample passage above, the notes would look like this:

Questions   **Answers**

Three types of rocks:
    sedimentary, metamorphic,
    igneous.

Sedimentary—sand, soil,
    broken rocks   settle in
    layers; compressed from
    the pressure of layers above
    them. Ex: sandstone,
    limestone

Igneous—formed by molten
    magma; rocks formed by
    cooling and hardening.
    Ex: obsidian, granite

Metamorphic—sedimentary
    with igneous melting by
    earth's heat; new rocks
    formed by cooling and
    hardening. Ex: marble,
    gneiss

Step 2: Add questions to the left-hand column. You can do this after taking all the notes for that chapter or section or as you take notes for each paragraph:

Questions	**Answers**
What are the three types of rocks?	Three types of rocks: sedimentary, metamorphic, igneous.
What is sedimentary rock?	Sedimentary—sand, soil, broken rocks settle in layers; compressed from the pressure of layers above them.
What are examples of sedimentary rock?	Ex: sandstone, limestone
What is igneous rock?	Igneous—formed by molten magma; rocks formed by cooling and hardening.
What are examples of igneous rock?	Ex: obsidian, granite
What are metamorphic rocks?	Metamorphic—sedimentary with igneous melting by earth's heat; new rocks formed by cooling and hardening.
What are examples of metamorphic rock?	Ex: marble, gneiss

The two-column note-taking technique is particularly useful for studying. You can fold the paper from the right margin to the middle of the page to cover the answers, leaving only the questions showing. Then read the questions and see if you can answer correctly. Open the folded paper to reveal your answers, and see if you covered all the points. If so, move on to the next question. If not, put a dot as a reminder to return to a question to try it again. After going through all the questions, review those which you marked with dots, erasing or crossing out the dot when you answer the question correctly. In this way you can avoid repeating the questions you already know and concentrate on those with which you had difficulty.

Right-Brain Note-Taking

Linear note-taking such as outlining and listing does not work well for right-brain people. They need to see the big picture or overview first. There are several techniques that work well for right-brain people that give them the total picture.

Technique 1: Right-Brain Two-Column Note-Taking

There is a way that right-brain people can benefit from two-column note-taking. The end result looks the same as the samples provided in the left-brain two-column note-taking section. The difference is in the process of arriving at the final result.

In right-brain two-column note-taking you first scan the chapter, looking for the key points, then list them first as questions in the left-hand column. You can find the key points by looking at the chapter headings, the subheadings, or the topics printed in bold, and any further subtopics. Sometimes a book offers an overview with key questions at the beginning of a chapter and a review or summary with key questions or points at the end of a chapter. These topics and key points will be written as questions in the left-hand column. The right side of the brain wants to know the total picture before starting a task. By searching for all the topics to be covered in a unit or chapter first, the right brain has a mind-set in which to place the details it will read as it goes along. Thus, it begins the chapter with a total picture. Then it will read as if searching for the answers to each question. The right side of the brain now has a purpose for reading. The details it finds will then fall into place in the framework it has already established.

This process works best when you have a text or book in which the topics are highlighted as titles and subtitles, or printed in bold or colored type. If the right-brain person has a choice of several books on the same topic, it is more helpful to choose one that has the chapters broken up by subtopics, bold headers, and key points to help you get the overview and thus make your note-taking easier. Sometimes, though, there are books which are pure text, paragraph after paragraph, which are not broken up by headers for topics and subtopics. These are more difficult for right-brain people because they have to scan each paragraph to find topics. Thus, in the passage above, about the three types of rocks, without subtitles, a right-brain person would have to scan it. They may come up with questions that look more like this:

Questions	**Answers**
What are three types of rocks?	
What is sedimentary rock?	
What is igneous rock?	
What is metamorphic rock?	

After listing all the questions, they will then read and write the answers in the right-hand column. Only after writing all the responses in the right-hand column can they see how to break their notes up further by making up more subquestions in the left-hand column. They may find that in writing the answer on the right they see there are some examples, and they may want to add a question such as, "What are some examples of sedimentary rock?" In some cases, they may feel there is no need to add questions, and will just respond to the main question on the left-hand side by using all the details on the right-hand side as one answer.

For studying, the right-brain person can also fold the paper from the right-hand edge to the middle of the page, covering the answers. Then they can ask the questions from the left-hand column and try to answer them, fold back the paper to uncover the answer, and check whether they replied correctly. They can put a dot next to questions they missed and return to them later. If they get them right on the second try, they can erase the dots or cross through them until they have answered all the missed questions correctly.

Technique 2: Right-Brain Mind-Mapping

Mind-mapping is a technique made popular by Tony Buzan in *Using Both Sides of the Brain* (New York: Dutton, 1977). He recommended this approach for taking notes. A mind-map is a diagram of the points of a subject in which the relationships between the information can be seen as a global overview. Other words for mind-mapping are: semantic webbing, webbing, or making graphic organizers. I used to teach the mind-mapping technique to everyone, only to find with dismay that the left-brain people continued to find more success in outlining, two-column note-taking, or making lists. Left-brain people learn better by using the left-brain linear, sequential approach, while right-brain people prefer mind-mapping techniques.

In its simplest form it looks like this:

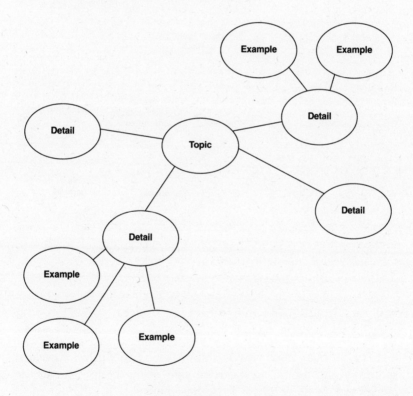

Use the same sample passage about the three types of rocks to make a mind map of the information. It may look something like this:

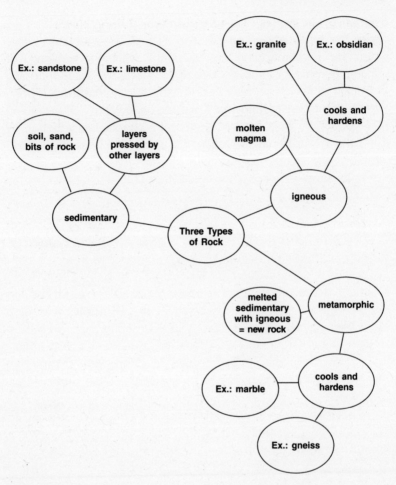

The above mind map shows the relationship between subtopics and topics, so the right side of the brain can see the global picture all at once. It is preferable that a different mind map be made for each new topic. If the page starts getting too crowded, you can make a separate mind map of each subtopic if there are many further subtopics and examples.

Using Left-Brain and Right-Brain Note-Taking Skills With Your Learning Style

Now that you have the basic note-taking techniques for left-brain and right-brain thinkers, we have to adapt them for the four types of learning styles: visual, auditory, tactile, and kinesthetic. You will use the note-taking technique that fits your left-brain or right-brain preference with the following additions based on your learning style:

Visual Learners: If you are left-brain you should use the left-brain outlining or left-brain two-column note-taking technique, writing the words neatly so that you have something to look at. If right-brain, you should use right-brain, two-column note-taking or the right-brain mind map, and add pictures, diagrams, or icons alongside your notes to get the pictorial images. If right-brain, you can use colored pens, pencils, or markers to set off the topics from the subtopics, or groups of topics. You may want to make artistically designed shapes in your mind map. Instead of circles, you may draw boxes, hearts, triangles, or free-flowing shapes. It is not the act of drawing or writing that is important to you, but being able to see the material on paper when you're reviewing it.

Auditory Learners: If you are left-brain, you should use left-brain outlining or left-brain, two-column note-taking and say the points aloud as you write them. When reviewing your notes you should read them aloud and talk about them out loud. If right-brain, you should use right-brain, two-column note-taking or right-brain mind-mapping and read the points aloud as you write them. When reviewing your notes, read and talk about them aloud. If right-brain, you can make verbal associations, mnemonics, or rhyming words to help you remember some of the ideas or key words.

Tactile Learners: If you are left-brain you should use the left-brain outlining or left-brain, two-column note-taking, writing the words because you recall what you write. If you are right-brain, you should use right-brain, two-column note-taking or the right-brain mind map, and draw pictures, diagrams, or icons alongside your notes because you will remember pictures that you drew. If you are right-brain you can use colored pens, pencils, or markers to set off the topics from the subtopics, or groups of topics. You can make your mind map in creative, artistic ways using different shapes and designs instead of circles. You may want to sketch drawings that are personally tied to your feelings to help you remember. It is the act of drawing and writing that helps the tactile learner remember the notes, not necessarily seeing them later. Many tactiles take copious notes but will never look at them again because they remember the material just by writing or drawing it.

Kinesthetic Learners: If you are left-brain, you should use the   left-brain   outlining   or   left-brain   two-column   note-taking method, using a larger pad so you can write the words larger, using your arm muscles instead of your finger muscles to write. If you are right-brain, you should use the right-brain, two-column note-taking method or the right-brain mind map, using a large-size paper so you can use your arm muscles to write rather than your fine hand muscles. You should add quick sketchy cartoonlike action pictures, diagrams, or icons alongside your notes because they will help you remember the action. If you are right brain, you can use colored pens, pencils, or markers to set off topics from subtopics, or groups of topics. You can make your mind map in creative, artistic ways using different shapes and designs. Make sure your drawings are action-oriented to help you remember the notes. It is the action of drawing and writing, using your muscles, that helps you remember, not necessarily seeing your notes later. You will recall what you *do*, not what you see.

Taking Notes From Verbal Presentations or Lectures, Audio-Visual Materials, Computers, Activities, and Real-Life Experiences

If you recall, we learn not only from books and written materials, but from other forms of media as well. We may learn from verbal presentations or lectures, from audio-visual materials, computers, activities, and real-life experiences. You will use the same note-taking processes as described in the above sections, matching your brain hemispheric preference and learning style. The following adjustments need to be made for each learning style:

Visual Learners: Because you need to see the material, you may find it more difficult to take notes from verbal presentations or lectures, audio materials, or activities and real-life experiences that do not supply visual information. Here are three techniques to help you:

1. Try to find printed or illustrated material, diagrams, graphs, or charts that cover the material and review these before hearing the verbal presentation. Take notes the day or night before the lecture or oral presentation and bring your notes to class. As the instructor lectures, follow your notes to see if you already wrote the material. If you did not, add the new information from the lecture to your notes in a different color so you will know which information was added by the instructor and which was from the book. In this way you can have something to look at during the lecture and can easily add anything that is new. This method requires you to find out in advance what will be covered the following day so you can stay ahead of the game.

2. The second technique involves taking dictation from the oral presentation. Even though you will be mindlessly writing down whatever is said, leaving out little words such as *the*, *an*, *these*, you will actually do your thinking later, on your own, as you read the "transcript" you have made of the lecture, comprehending it, and then transferring it into your particular note-taking style. It is hard for you to follow a lecture without visuals, so the best chance you have of "getting it" is by just continuing to write and then reading the notes back at home, doing your experiential comprehension and memory techniques to under-

stand and remember them. Then convert your dictation into your note-taking format.

3. Ask the instructor to write an outline on the board to accompany the lecture, or ask for a printed handout of the study guide for each lecture. Then you can follow that, adding in points as you go along.

Auditory Learners: You do well with verbal presentations such as lectures or audio-visual material that has a sound component, and find it easy to take notes from these media. If there is no talking involved in the activities or real-life experiences, then you will need to ask questions to have the facilitator provide you with explanations of what is happening or talk it through with a partner so you can write what is said in note-taking format. You may need to find written material or study guides related to the activities and real-life experiences so you can read them aloud and then take notes on them. Having these will function as an auditory experience for you, making the material easy to follow. You can read aloud, whisper-read, tape-record yourself reading it aloud or tape someone else, or listen to the words in your head as you take notes.

Tactile Learners: Since you learn best by writing, drawing, or doing hands-on activities, taking notes is easy for you. You will recall activities and real-life experiences because these are often hands-on activities, and you can just jot down a few notes to remind you of the activity you did. Your difficulty often lies in auditory presentations. Here are some techniques to help you take notes in different situations:

1. Like the visual learner, you may just have to take dictation as fast as you can, slowly read it back when alone, and convert it into your own form of note-taking to match your learning style.

2. You will probably do better at auditory presentations if the instructor lectures on a specific reading. From the printed text, you can take notes the night before and bring them to class. In

this way, instead of writing everything that is said in the lecture you can find what you already wrote and then only add the new material. You may want to write the lecture notes in a different color than you used for the notes from the text, so if the instructor says you will be tested on the textbook, you can study the notes in that color. If the instructor says you will be tested on the lecture notes, then you can study the notes you took in that color.

In some classes, such as English literature, discussions may not be based on specific details of the plot, but on higher-level critical thinking abilities such as comparing and contrasting, discussing a theme, or evaluating a character's actions. If that is the case and you know the type of discussion you will have in class, you should read the material beforehand to understand the plot and then make a mind map or chart of other elements such as the theme, characters' motives, author's purposes, or comparing and contrasting different elements of the text. In this way you can be prepared with notes that will help you in class discussions.

3. If there is a lecture or audio-visual material, you can ask the instructor for a study guide, or request that notes be put on the board so you can copy them during the lecture or while the audio-visual material is playing.

Kinesthetic Learners: Since you learn best by doing, you will recall activities and real-life experiences by writing a few notes to trigger your memory of the event. You will find more difficulty with written materials, auditory presentations, and audio-visual materials that do not have motion. Here are some techniques to help you take notes in these situations:

1. Since you already learned experiential comprehension and how to convert written material into action in Chapter 21, your best shot is to get hold of printed material. If you are faced with an auditory presentation or lecture, get a book or textbook on the subject and read it the night or day before the lecture,

taking notes from the text. Then bring your notes to class and follow them, actively looking for the material mentioned in the lecture. Think of it as a game or puzzle in which you have to find what you already wrote and add in what is new, preferably in a different color. See how many notes you took already and how many the instructor is adding. In this way you are actually *doing* something during the lecture and will not be overwhelmed by all the talking because you already took notes in your kinesthetic style the night before.

2. If you can't get hold of the text you will have to take dictation, writing down everything the instructor says so that you can later convert it into your kinesthetic experiential comprehension and memory techniques. Do not worry if you cannot comprehend as the instructor talks—just write everything down, thinking of it as a challenge or competition to keep up with the instructor. Then convert the material into a kinesthetic note-taking approach later by going over the "transcript" of the lecture.

3. Ask the instructor to provide a study guide or notes on the board that you can add to when the instructor presents anything new. This will make it easier for you to follow an auditory or audio-visual presentation.

In the exercise below, try out the note-taking techniques appropriate to your brain hemispheric preference and your learning style. After you find out which of the techniques you prefer, begin taking notes on the subject you selected for your field of study as you work through the book. With a little bit of practice, taking notes will become second nature and you will accelerate your learning.

EXERCISE: Using the subject you are studying as you work through this book, select a passage and take notes from it using your brain hemispheric preference and your learning style. Try both of the techniques given for your brain hemispheric preference to see which one you prefer.

Study Skills

Study skills are the strategies you use to review what you learned in preparation for a test, performance assessment, or for using the material in real-life activities. It is a review session in which you go over the material to trigger your memory. In the review process you are assessing which portions of the material you know and which ones you still do not know and will have to relearn or clarify. One problem that many people have with study time is that this is often the first time they've tried to learn the material. Study should be a *review* of what you learned, not a chance to learn something for the first time. I see many students who come to me to "study for a test," only to discover that they never learned the material in the first place. If you find you have to learn months of material in hours, the best you could do the night before an exam is to use the experiential comprehension technique for your learning link and the memory techniques. The quantity you can study then depends on how many pages you have to cover and the time allotted to you before the test.

We must reframe our thoughts about studying. Do not leave learning for the night or even week before a test. Learning must go on continually, with the appropriate method of note-taking. Study time should be reserved for reviewing the notes that trigger what is already in your memory. It involves the following steps:

1. Using your notes for review: If you take notes, you have less to look over than if you had to review an entire textbook. Whereas a textbook may take several hours to several days or weeks to review, the notes may take anywhere from only a few minutes to several hours.

2. Sorting out the portions of your notes you already know from those that you are not sure of or have forgotten: If you used the two-column, note-taking technique, you can cover the answers on the right side of the page, ask yourself the questions on the left side, and then uncover the answers to see which questions you answered correctly. Put dots next to the questions you need to review. If you used a mind-map approach, review what is on it, then turn the mind-map face down and see how much of it you can recall. Put dots next to the parts of the mind-map that you forgot and spend time going over them.

3. Going over those portions you are not sure of or have forgotten: After doing step two, you will be left with the questions you answered incorrectly or the parts of the mind map that you don't remember. Review them and test yourself again. If you still do not grasp them, it could be that you did not understand that material the first time or your notes are not clear enough to trigger your memory. In this case you may have to go back to your textbook or notes of the lecture and redo that portion of your notes to make them clearer. You may have to look up some terminology in a glossary or dictionary to make it clearer. Do this until you are able to answer the questions accurately.

4. Checking your understanding of the terminology: You may want to highlight or make a separate list of terms or vocabulary you need to know. The two-column approach is ideal for this because you can quiz yourself by covering the definition. List the words in the left-hand column and the definition in the right-hand column. Mark the words you miss and spend more time on those. You may have to make a stronger word association, as described in the chapter on memory, to help you remember better. Go over the dotted words until you get them correct.

5. For performance tasks, do practice activities and measure your performance against your goals: In certain fields it is not so much a question of memorizing information than of performing a task or a process. Examples would be: math, chemistry, cooking, surgery, car repair, driving, basketball, gymnastics, construction, public speaking, writing, and architectural design. Studying for these types of performance tests means practicing the task. Your notes can guide you through the process, but you will have to practice the task on your own to gain proficiency in it. As you do it, measure your performance against the required standards and rework those sections with which you have difficulty. Try to have someone else who can guide you review your performance. Try not to leave practice for the night before—leave enough time to get help in the areas you identify as being weak. After getting help, continue to work on those portions that need improvement until you are satisfied that you meet the performance standards.

How Long Should You Study?

You need to study until you master the material. For some it may be minutes, for others, hours or days. Do not set a certain amount of time as your goal; rather, make mastering the material your objective. Here are some helpful hints:

1. Review the material after taking notes on it.
2. Look over the previous day's notes as a refresher before starting the current day's notes.
3. At the end of the week, review all the notes for that week.
4. At the beginning of the next week, review the previous week's notes.
5. At the end of each month, review the notes for the past month.
6. Before the test, spend one week reviewing all the notes, section by section, so you see all your notes at least one more time before the test.
7. The night before the test, review all the notes. If time is short, review only those that you had dotted as trouble spots.

8. On the morning of the test, review all the notes, or sometime during the day of the test again review the remaining dotted notes that were trouble spots.

9. If the test is not the final exam and you know the material will come up again on the final examination or a qualifying, entrance, or proficiency exam, continue to review the notes once a month until the test. In the month before the test, review everything again, bit by bit. In the final week before the test, review all the trouble spots again. The night before the test, review all the dotted sections, or trouble spots, one more time.

Remember, this study time gives you a chance to use and retrieve what is already in your memory by keeping the information active as long as you need it to pass a test or performance examination, or to use it on the job.

EXERCISE: Use the notes you were taking at the beginning of this chapter for the subject you are learning, and practice studying them using the techniques described in this section. Look them over, cover them up, and see if you can recall the notes. Check your response against the written notes to see which areas you know and which you still need to study. Make a timetable for yourself, entering the time of day you will spend each day studying the notes you have taken.

Test-Taking Skills

Test-taking skills involve two steps: preparing for the test and actually taking it. Although this section deals with traditional paper-pencil tests and how to prepare for and take them, the concepts can be applied to performance assessments. While your preparation will be more in the area of practice, you can prime yourself for the task by knowing what you will be assessed on, practicing, and knowing how your performance will be measured and what you will be expected to do at the time of assessment.

Preparing for the Test

Test-preparation includes the skills we already learned: comprehension, memory, note-taking, and study skills, plus a few additional tasks to get you ready for a test. If you have done your experiential comprehension, memory activities, note- taking, and used your appropriate study skills you have won most of the battle. But there are a few more tasks to prepare for the test that are not covered by the above skills:

1. Find out what is on the test: You may be well prepared for what you thought would be on the test, only to discover there are items on it you did not know were going to be there. You say to yourself, "If I knew that was on the test, I would have studied for that and would have passed." When I analyze the test results of students I worked with I find that they knew everything about the topics I helped them study. The questions they missed were items they didn't realize they had to know. The first and most important step in test preparation is to know what the test will cover. How can you find that out? Easy— ask. There are only two possible replies when you ask the instructor what is on the test: "You should know this, this, and this," and then you can take notes on all the items mentioned, or he or she will say, "Know everything!" in which case you will have to study all the written texts, class notes, and activities— everything.

Your test-preparation should begin with making a chart, graph, diagram, list, or mind map, depending on your learning style, noting the items to be covered on the test.

2. Organize your study materials: You need to organize your notes, lecture materials, written materials, study guides, handouts, and everything else related to each item that will be tested. Then if you find you are missing material you have time to get it from the instructor or other participants in the class. If you missed a portion of the class, you should find out what was covered during your absence and get the materials for that section.

3. Make a time management chart including the date and time of the test, and all the time you have available for study: Prepare a calendar or time management chart (see diagram below). Figure out how much material you need to review and study. If you took good notes you can count the number of units or sections in which your notes are divided and determine how many you have to review before the test. Then you can decide how many units you need to study each day to reach your goal. For example:

History: Time: 3 weeks before the test, or 21 days
Units: 6 units of study, or 6 groups of notes needing
              2 hours each

$$\begin{array}{r} 3.5 \\ 6\overline{)21} \end{array}$$ or 21 days divided by 6 units = 3 1/2 days for
                                                           each unit

This tells you that for each unit you can spend two hours spread out over three and a half days of studying to cover all the topics before the test.

Here is what your time management calendar could look like:

Days	Sun.	Mon.	Tues.	Wed.	Thurs.	Fri.	Sat.
	1 Chapter 1—1 hour	2 Chapter 1—1/2 hour	3 Chapter 1—1/4 hour	4 Chapter 1—1/4 hour Chapter 2—1/4 hour	5 Chapter2—1/2 hour	6 Chapter 2—1/2 hour	7 Chapter 2—3/4 hour. Chapter 3—1/2 hour
	8 Day off	9 Chapter 3—1 hour	10 Chapter 3—1/2 hour	11 Chapter 4—1/2 hour	12 Chapter 4—1 hour	13 Day off	14 Chapter 4—1/2 hour. Chapter 5—2 hours.
	15 Chapter 6—2 hours	16 Chapters 1 and 2 trouble areas	17 Chapters 2 and 4 trouble areas	18 Chapters 5 and 6 trouble areas	19 Chapters 1-6, all trouble areas	20 Chapters 1-6, all trouble areas	21 **Day of the Test**

By making calendars or time charts you can make sure you leave enough time to cover all the material in preparation for the test.

4. Try to take a practice test simulating the actual test as closely as possible: You may be perfectly prepared for the material to be tested, but get thrown off because the format of the questions is unfamiliar. For example, you may have been prepared for multiple-choice questions only to find that it is a fill-in-the-blank or essay test. Ask in advance what the format of the test will be. Then you can do practice activities from your textbooks, work sheets, or practice pages that match the format.

5. Know the strategies for the types of test questions: If you have followed all the steps in this book so far—experiential comprehension, memory techniques, note-taking skills, and study skills—you should know the material thoroughly. You should know it as well as the instructor and have the entire textbook or course material in your head. Thus, no question should stump you because you fully understand and comprehend the subject. You should be able to answer a question whether it is a multiple-choice, fill-in-the-blank, matching, true or false, or essay question. Even if you know the material, the format of the question can have hidden pitfalls that throw you off. You need to understand the strategies involved in answering each type of question and be prepared for them. Doing practice activities using the format that will be used on the test can prepare you so that you do not have to waste time during the test figuring out how to respond.

6. Get in the right state of mind before the test: If you think back to the chapter in this book on preparation for learning (chapter 19), you may recall that you need to be in a relaxed state. If you are afraid, your higher-thinking centers may shut down, leaving you in the instinctive fight-or-flight part of the brain. You want to go into the test in a relaxed state so that your higher brain is working. Here are some things you can do to keep your mental attitude positive:

a. Relax: Do relaxation exercises each night during the week before the test, such as deep-breathing exercises to get the oxygen flowing to your brain. Relax your muscles. Do meditation to be in a calm and peaceful state of mind. Listen to relaxing music. Use any of the techniques that you have been using in preparation for learning.

b. Visualize success: Spend a few minutes each day before the test visualizing yourself succeeding on it. See yourself answering the questions with confidence and ease. Imagine yourself getting a perfect paper. The visual learners will see this, the auditories will hear themselves saying that they were successful, the tactiles will feel their success, and the kinesthetics will experience themselves going up to the instructor to pick up their successful papers.

c. Make positive affirmations or statements every day for a week before the test. If you have done all the steps described in this book, you are well prepared. Here are some examples of affirmations you can make: "I am ready for this test." "I have studied everything and know everything there is to know for this test." "I know everything that is in the book for this test." "I know everything the instructor knows for this test." "I am a good student." "I am a winner."

Taking the Test

If you have done all the steps laid out in this book so far, the test is actually anticlimatic. Your work is done. Your mind is filled with everything you need to know to succeed. You are in a relaxed, confident frame of mind. You have already taken the test in your mind through visualization and have passed. On the day of the test you are merely going through the motions. It will be a breeze because you have already learned the subject, memorized it, practiced it, reviewed it, and have your mind set to do well. You just need to remember to do the following things while taking the test:

1. Read the directions as carefully as you had studied the material, using your experiential comprehension. Understand each word of the directions and see, hear, feel, or experience yourself doing every step of the directions so you do not miss a word. In your mind, make a movie of yourself following the directions exactly.

2. Read each question and the choices carefully, using your experiential comprehension. Make a movie in your mind of what the questions and choices are saying. Do not miss any details. Do not jump to conclusions. Read every word and make an image for each word. Only when you are clear about the question and choices should you proceed to answer the question.

3. Stay relaxed so you are in your higher-thinking part of the brain. If you feel any fear or nervousness, take some deep breaths, or take a few seconds to meditate to stay relaxed.

4. If you find a hard question, mark a dot next to it and return to it. Do not waste time on hard questions, but in each section do all the ones you know first and return to the hard questions at the end. Spending time on one hard question can cost you four or five shorter questions. Often, after doing the easier questions the harder ones become easier as well.

5. Pace yourself. If there are longer questions or essay questions, decide how much time you want to spend on the shorter questions and how much time you need to leave for the longer ones. Move quickly but do not rush. Missing important words could throw you off.

6. If there is time left over, return to check your answers. Do not haphazardly change your answers. Remember, you have thought through and analyzed your choices, so you were probably right the first time around. Only change an answer if you know you guessed the first time around without analyzing. Do the analysis first, eliminating poor choices, and then change the answer only if you can prove that the new choice is the correct one.

7. Trust your memory. You spent a lot of time converting everything you learned into a movie in your mind based on your

learning style. Your memory in your best learning style is excellent. When you rerun those memories in your learning style the answers are there. Trust them.

EXERCISE: Option 1: If you are taking a course concurrently in the subject that you are using to work through this book, use the techniques in this chapter to prepare for a test, if one is coming up.

Option 2: If you are not currently taking a course that has a test, find a book or workbook on the subject that you are studying that has a practice test, chapter review checkup, or a quiz. Use it as a practice test for this exercise. See what is on the test and do the activities in this chapter to prepare for the "test."

For both Option 1 and Option 2: Make a timetable for studying for the test. Fix the date for the test, analyze how much material you need to review, and then fill in the calendar. Get used to doing this for upcoming tests so that you leave yourself enough time to study. Remember, study time is only for *reviewing* what you have already learned—not for *learning* a subject!

Now you know the secrets to learning anything quickly and accurately.

24

Applying What You've Learned

In the beginning of this book you selected a subject to learn as you worked through the activities. You also had a goal or purpose for learning that subject. Think back to what that goal was. If you worked through all of these topics you would be well on your way to mastering your subject by using the tools provided in this book. Applying what you learned to your life can be a stepping stone to personal transformation and the attainment of your dreams.

Many people think of learning as a dead-end road. They learn something and that is the end of it. Few people actually *use* what they learn. Many people take courses and never apply the material or skills they've learned to their lives. Twelve years of schooling, possibly sixteen or more if we go to training schools or colleges, have conditioned us into taking courses, passing tests, and forgetting the material the following day. As a society we have come to equate learning with passing tests and getting grades, diplomas, or certificates. But the true nature of learning is a transformation into a better self, a higher self, a fully developed self. As a by-product we can put what we learned into the service of humanity at large and make the world a better place. Learning is a tool that helps us achieve our goals and dreams.

The final step in accelerated learning is applying what we learned to our everyday lives. That is the best and fastest way to crown our learning, to ensure our mastery of a subject. Having reached the point where we have mastered a subject, we want to gain experience by applying what we learned to real-life situations. By doing so we move forward on our life's journey to meet the goals we have set for ourselves.

If we are learning a skill for a current job or hobby, we are most likely going to apply what we learned on a regular basis. If we have learned a new subject unrelated to our current activities, the following are some examples of how we can apply these to everyday life:

Literature: Continue to read on your own; start a discussion group; keep a journal; and do your own writing.

Sports or dance: Find some friends or join a group to practice a sport or dance.

Using the Internet: Spend time daily "surfing" to locate web sites related to your fields of interest.

Carpentry: Start a small project, building something for your home.

Cooking: Invite friends over for a gourmet meal.

Marketing: Find a product your business produces and improve on marketing it.

Health: Set some personal health goals in the areas of diet, nutrition, fitness, or exercise; start a personal program for yourself or join a fitness club.

Quantum Physics: Find a laboratory to visit or work in, either part-time or as a volunteer so you can apply what you learned to research.

Learning is more than studying for a test. Having passed our examinations or performance assessments and proven our knowledge of a subject or skill, we do not want to have wasted all that time and let our knowledge fade away with disuse. True, there may be subjects we had to take that we had no use for. Focus instead on those subjects that you chose to study as part of your life's work, goals, interests, hobbies, or talents. The process of accelerated learning is complete when we use what we learned right away.

In the past, learners used to do numerous practice activities, yet did not recall the subject when they were assessed months later because they did not apply what they learned. When they used their knowledge and skills in everyday life the material stayed in their long-term memories. The final stage in accelerated learning is to use what you learn in your daily life.

One of the best ways to apply what you learn about a subject is to teach it to others. To teach, you must digest the subject, make it a part of you, and then explain it to others. By doing so you can become an expert in the field. Take the subject you have studied and try to teach it to someone else. Instruction does not have to be formal. You can share what you have learned with a family member, friend, child, or coworker who is interested in the same subject. Find out their learning link and try to teach it to them in their best style.

Accelerated Learning Begins Early

We have a misconception in our society that the very young and very old are living in a state in which they are unaware of what is happening around them. We let children lie in cribs or baby carriages for hours, unstimulated with no one to talk to them, no one to provide them with challenges, or no one to expose them to life. For each hour they lie awake doing nothing they lose an hour of learning time. It is the same with the elderly who are left to sit with nothing to do.

Learning begins at birth. When we expose children to mental stimuli in infancy and their toddler years, we help them develop talents and abilities early. From infancy, we can develop their whole brain, both left and right sides, and all four learning styles by exposing them to a rich environment filled with stimuli in each modality. We need not wait until age five, when they enter kindergarten. As a society we need to extend education to infancy, training parents and communities to provide opportunities for early stimulation. Having worked with gifted students, I found the one common thread in each of their upbringings was that their parents provided them with early language experiences, early reading experiences, and a wide range of experiences in math, science, music, art, sports, hobbies, and talents. If we teach young people how to learn in an accelerated way we will see a nation of students who are ready for higher-level work at earlier ages instead of finding upper-grade students and adults dropping out of society because no one has taught them *how* to learn.

Maturity Is No Barrier to Learning

Just as young people can be trained in the methods of accelerated learning, so can senior citizens. Studies have shown that our brain does not decline after retirement. Millions of people over sixty-five have been led to believe that their days of learning are over. Earlier in the book you read that increased stimulation develops increased interconnections among nerve cells in the brain, which are necessary for continued brain growth and development. That development continues all through life. It is society that promotes the false belief that our development is over when we retire.

We do not have to stop learning when we graduate from school or retire. Learning can be a lifelong pursuit, bringing with it new skills, interests, hobbies, talents, and contributions to the lives of people around us and the world. We can take continuing education courses and master them at an accelerated pace, or we can plan an accelerated program of self-study using the tools in this book. Live each day as the beginning of a new life. Age is an illusion. Decide to wake up each day as fresh and vibrant as you did as a child, teen, or young adult, looking forward to your entire life ahead of you. Many gifted writers, scientists, artists, in-

ventors, musicians, and craftspeople began their careers after
sixty or seventy. You can too!

Transforming Yourself and the World

Now that your studies are over, you have time freed up so you
can put what you learned to use. Can you help yourself with that
knowledge? Can you help someone else? Can you use it at your
job? Can you use it to help your family? Can you use it to solve
a problem in your community, nation, or the world?

EXERCISE: Think about the subject you chose to learn as you
worked through the book. List all the ways that you can apply
what you learned to your daily life, using what you learned for
your personal transformation, to help others, or to transform the
world.

You have invested time in reading this book and working
through it. You are now ready to apply these accelerated learning
techniques to any other field. The appendix contains examples of
how to apply the accelerated learning plan to various subjects as
ways to get you started.

Share the knowledge and technology you learned with others in your family, workplace, or educational institution. By using
these tools to learn anything quickly, you can accelerate your
progress, work towards your own personal transformation, and
begin to transform the world.

Appendix: How to Use Your Superlink in Different Fields of Learning

As you embark on your lifelong learning plan, you may encounter a variety of fields that you must learn. This section illustrates how you can apply what you learned about your superlink and accelerated learning to master different subjects. The sample applications are in both academic and performance fields: math, writing, technical reading (computer manuals), sciences, sports or dance, vocational fields, and hobbies. For each subject, adaptations for each learning link are provided, giving you the strategy to accelerate your learning in that field.

Math

Visual Left-Brain	Look at the numbers and the problem. Read the directions written out in words in a step-by-step way. You will remember the steps to solving the problem if they are accompanied by a written description of the numerical steps.
Visual Right-Brain	Look at the numbers and the problem in its entirety, with the answer. The problem must be accompanied by a graphic illustration to demonstrate it. The graphics can be in the form of pictures, charts, diagrams, photographs, or real objects. Several examples of the same type of problem, complete with answers, need to be seen so the right side of the brain can "see" the repeating pattern of the formula in order to understand it.
Auditory Left-Brain	Talk through the problem in a step-by-step way. Listen to a verbal explanation of each of its steps.
Auditory Right-Brain	Look at the numbers and the problem with accompanying pictorial, real-life examples, written out in a global way, complete with answers, and then talk through the problem. Talk through and look at pictorial examples of the same type of problem, with the answers, to understand the mathematical pattern.
Tactile Left-Brain	Write down the numbers and the problem in a step-by-step way. Write the written explanations or directions for doing the problem. Use hands-on manipulatives to accompany the written directions. Relate the problems to feelings. Work with someone you like.

Tactile Right-Brain	Write out the numbers and the whole problem with the answers, accompanied by drawings or sketches to illustrate the problem. Use hands-on manipulatives to accompany the written problem. Write out several samples of the same type of problem, with the answers, to understand the mathematical pattern. Connect feelings to the problem. Work with people you like.
Kinesthetic Left-Brain	Physically act out problems using concrete real-life examples in a game, simulation, or role-play in a step-by-step way and talk about it. Write the numbers in large size while standing up at a board or flip chart and talk through the problem in a step-by-step way. Use sports or game equipment, physical exercise, or movement as a bonus for working out each problem in order to keep actively engaged.
Kinesthetic Right-Brain	Physically act out the problem with concrete, real-life examples in a global way, with the answer. Do several examples of the same type of problem, with the answers, so the right side of the brain can understand the pattern of how to do it. Use large manipulatives to illustrate the problem. Write the numbers and the problem in large size while standing at a board or flip chart. Play sports, games, or do a physical activity while practicing the problem. Keep your body physically engaged as you work through problems.

Writing

Visual Left-Brain	Plan your writing using a left-brain outline. See all parts of the written piece first before attempting to write. Use a graphic organizer in a step-by-step way to see all the parts of the written piece. The organizer should contain a checklist to go over to make sure all the components essential for good writing have been included. After writing the piece, go through an evaluative checklist to make sure your writing has a focus, details and examples to support the topic, logical organization, and correct mechanics. Keep a chart with a checklist to help you see whether your piece is organized. You can check off each item as you go through it so you can see what you have done correctly and what you need to do more work on.
Visual Right-Brain	Write a mind map of the piece to use as a plan before doing the actual writing. After writing the piece following your mind map, have a checklist in mind-map form to evaluate the piece and make sure all components are included. (See components for an evaluative checklist in the visual left-brain section above.) Using the mind map helps the visual right-brain person see what should be included in a written piece.
Auditory Left-Brain	Use the left-brain outline as described in the visual left-brain section, but talk through each part. After writing the piece, read each portion of the checklist aloud to evaluate the written piece. Reread the piece aloud to see if the components in the evaluative checklist have been covered.

Auditory Right-Brain	Use the right-brain mind map as described in the visual right-brain section above, but talk through each part aloud. After writing the piece, read each portion of the mind map checklist aloud to evaluate the piece. Reread the written piece aloud to see if the components in the evaluative checklist have been covered.
Tactile Left-Brain	Write the outline for a written piece using the left-brain outline format as described in the visual left-brain section above. Relate the piece to your feelings. After writing the piece, write the components of the evaluative checklist and place a check mark for each item contained in the piece. Rewrite the piece to include any of the missing components.
Tactile Right-Brain	Plan the written piece by drawing a mind map and filling in each bubble with topics, subtopics, and examples. Relate the piece to your own feelings. After writing the piece using the mind-map plan, evaluate it using the mind-map checklist. Underline or highlight in color the portions that need reworking. Rewrite those portions until all components have been included in the written piece.
Kinesthetic Left-Brain	On a flip chart or chalkboard, write an outline for a written piece using the left-brain outline format as described in the visual left-brain section above. Visualize yourself doing the actions in each part of the story. If possible, role-play what you want to write about. Mount an evaluative checklist on a board, stand up, and using your arm muscles place a check mark for each item contained in the piece.

| **Kinesthetic Right-Brain** | Plan out the piece by completing the mind map as described in the visual right-brain section above, except write it in large size on a flip chart or chalkboard. Visualize yourself doing the actions involved in each portion of the story. If possible, physically act out or role-play what you want to write about. After writing the piece, mount the evaluative mind-map checklist on a board. Stand up and read your piece aloud, using your large arm muscles to check off each item from the checklist that you have covered. Rewrite the piece to ensure that all components are covered. |

Technical Reading

Visual Left-Brain	Technical reading is easy for you to understand. Reading words, ideas, and numbers written in a step-by-step way comes naturally to you. Since this is the visual format of technical material, it is compatible with your learning link.
Visual Right-Brain	You will need to see graphic illustrations to accompany the technical readings. Graphs, charts, diagrams, drawings, photographs, or real-life examples are a must for you to understand the reading. If there are none, you will need to do experiential visual right-brain reading, taking each sentence and converting it into a drawing or illustration. Since you have a hard time following the step-by-step directions involved in technical reading, you need to read through the introduction and the summary of the technical manual and look at all the topics and headings first to get an overview of what the manual contains. Make a schematic diagram in mind-map form of the topics first, and then, as you read, fill in the detail bubbles connected to each topic so you will have an overview of the entire manual. Use color to highlight different sections. Make an attractive poster or flow chart so you can refer to the steps in the reading at a glance.
Auditory Left-Brain	Read the technical material aloud in a step-by-step way. Technical manual is written in a left-brain way that appeals to your left brain, so reading it aloud puts it into your best mode of learning. You may wish to discuss or explain the steps to someone else so you can hear it aloud and remember it better.
Auditory Right-Brain	You will need to make a mind map of the technical reading and talk about the main points.

	To do this, go through the introduction and conclusion of the technical reading as well as look at the headings and topics first. Include these in the mind map and then, as you read the details of each, add them as bubbles connected to the main ideas. Try to enact the steps with the real objects or materials as you read. You will probably be tempted to just jump in and do the activities described in the technical reading first and fix any mistakes by trial and error, referring to the manual when necessary. If this is the case, do the activities first, and then go through the technical manual to refine your skills and make sure you have not missed anything important to the task.
Tactile Left-Brain	As you read the manual, copy down the instructions in a step-by-step way. Taking notes will help you learn it. If possible, *as you read*, use your hands to work on the equipment or machinery being described in the instructions. For example, if the manual describes steps to be done on a computer or equipment, as you read each step, perform the action on the equipment. Try to involve your feelings by having a purpose for doing the task that is meaningful to you. If possible, work with someone you like as you learn it.
Tactile Right-Brain	As you read the technical material, make a mind map with sketches, drawings, and diagrams of what you are learning. Use colors and designs to make the mind map. Draw a schematic diagram of what you need to do. Before beginning, get the global picture, or overview, of the entire process by looking at the introduction, conclusion, and main headings throughout the task. Use these as the main points in your mind map. Then fill in the details connected to the main point as you read. If possible, use your hands to work on the equipment as you go along. As you read each portion, enact

	the process with your hands on the actual tools or equipment. Try to involve your feelings in the process by having a motivation, or reason, for reading the material. If possible, work with someone you like as you learn.
Kinesthetic Left-Brain	Perform the actions described in the reading in a step-by-step way as you read. Read while working on the actual equipment or tools. Make a large left-brain outline on a flip chart or board as you read, while standing up. Talk through the steps as you perform them. Wherever possible, relate the material to actually performing the task.
Kinesthetic Right-Brain	Look over the material, focusing on the introduction and the conclusion and the main headings before reading. Look at any diagrams, pictures, or charts first. As you go through the technical manual, make a large mind map on a flip chart or large board while standing up, sketching out the main points with pictures and key words. For best results, physically perform the task as you read. You will probably want to jump right in and do it, learning by trial and error. You can do so, but refer to the technical reading to make sure you are heading in the right direction.

The Sciences

While each discipline has its own tradition, any subject can be adapted to be compatible to each of the superlinks. There are many fields of science, but two of the common characteristics in learning each of them are: reading the research of others, and experimenting by forming hypotheses and testing them using the scientific method. These processes can be adapted for each of the superlinks so that anyone using any learning link can be successful in the sciences.

Visual Left-Brain	Read the data or research in a text. For experiments, follow step-by-step directions as written in books or printed in charts. Keep organized charts of your experiments.
Visual Right-Brain	Look at illustrations, pictures, diagrams, photographs, or watch live demonstrations. Use texts that are accompanied by graphic illustrations. When performing experiments, use pictorial charts and diagrams or flow charts of the tasks. Icons and symbols will help you see, at a glance, the steps you need to perform. Look at the whole picture of the task before beginning so you can see the sequential steps in their larger context. Color-code equipment or graphs to help you follow steps in order. If possible, watch someone do the experiment so you have a visual model of what needs to be done.
Auditory Left-Brain	Read the research aloud and discuss it with others. Talk through the steps of an experiment first and as you are doing it. Try to work with others so you can discuss your ideas as you work. Tape-record or use a Dictaphone to record your results as you go along and play it back to think through the experiment.

Auditory Right-Brain	You will need to make a mind map of the scientific readings and write down the key points. Get a global overview of the entire process before beginning. To do this, go through the introduction, conclusion, headings, and topics first. Talk about the main points, preferably with others. Talk through the experiment as you do it. Enact the steps with the actual objects or materials. It is ideal to have someone to talk to as you do the experiment. If this isn't possible, use a tape recorder or Dictaphone to record what you do in the experiment and play it back later. You may want to jump in and do the experiment first, learning by trial and error, adjusting it as you go along.
Tactile Left-Brain	As you read science material, copy down notes in a step-by-step way: You learn by writing. Write your plan for your experiment in a step-by-step way first. Use your hands to do the experiment as you read your plan. Write your results in a step-by-step way. Try to involve your feelings by finding a purpose that is meaningful to you in doing the task. If possible, work with someone you like as you learn it.
Tactile Right-Brain	As you read science material, make a mind map with sketches, drawings, and diagrams of what you are learning. Use colors and designs in making the mind map. Draw a schematic diagram of what you need to do. Before beginning, get the global picture, or overview, of the entire process by looking at the introduction, conclusion, and main headings throughout the task. Use these as the main points in your mind map, then fill in the details connected to the main point as you read. If possible, use your hands to do the experiment rather than watch others. Before beginning an experiment, draw or sketch out what you plan to do. Make sketches, drawings,

	diagrams, or charts of the results. Use color and design. Try to involve your feelings in the process. If possible, work with someone you like as you learn.
Kinesthetic Left-Brain	As you read scientific material, visualize yourself sequentially doing the actions described. If possible, physically perform the actions described in the reading in a step-by-step way as you read. Read while working on the actual science equipment. Plan your experiment by making a large left-brain outline on a flip chart or board as you read, while standing up. Talk through the steps aloud as you perform them. Wherever possible, relate the material to the actual performance of the task. While standing up, keep a record of what you have done by making a large chart on a board. To make the experiment more active and lively, you will do well to work with a group.
Kinesthetic Right-Brain	Look over the material, focusing on the introduction and the conclusion and the main headings before reading. Look at any diagrams, pictures, or charts first. As you go through the readings, make a large mind map on a flip chart or board while standing up, sketching out the main points with pictures and key words, and then draw or sketch out your plan for the experiment. Use color, symbols, and icons wherever possible. Do the experiment and record the results in a mind map on a flip chart, with sketches. You will probably want to jump right in and do it, learning by trial and error. You can do so, but double-check to make sure you are working in the right direction. You will do well to work in a group setting, making learning more active and lively.

Sports or Dance

Visual Left-Brain	Read written instructions on how to perform the sport or dance. Enact each step as you read. The instructions should describe every small detail of movement required to perform the sport or dance successfully. Watch yourself in a mirror so you can check your performance against your own model.
Visual Right-Brain	Look at illustrations, pictures, diagrams, photographs, or watch live demonstrations of the sport or dance. See the entire process first, before going into each step. Find illustrations that show each movement of the sport or dance. Photographs are better than videos unless you stop the action of each video so you can get a clear view of each step. Watch yourself in a mirror so you can check your performance. You can also videotape yourself performing and compare it to the performer or instructor in the instructional video.
Auditory Left-Brain	First you need to hear each step of the direction. Then talk through the steps as you do them. Make sure they are broken down into every single movement you are required to do. For example, "Put your left foot forward six inches. Lift the heel of your right foot." Try to work with others so you can discuss the steps and movements. Tape-record or use a Dictaphone to record the instructions given by others so you can play them back until you remember them.
Auditory Right-Brain	Observe someone performing the entire sport or dance to get a global overview of the process. Have them describe a few key movements using a few sensory words. Tape-record these instructions so you can play them back. Turn on the music and jump in and perform the steps, getting them by trial and error. Talk through the key points of the steps with someone. Have someone observe you and tell you

	in a few simple sensory words how to adjust your performance.
Tactile Left-Brain	In a step-by-step way, write down the instructions that you read, hear, or observe, making sure you write down each detailed movement your body will have to do. Then enact each step with your body, following your written notes. Get your feelings involved in the sport or dance. Try to work with someone you like.
Tactile Right-Brain	Watch someone do the entire process of the sport or dance first. Then make sketches or drawings of the movements you will have to do. Follow your drawings as you perform the movement. Try to involve your feelings in the process. To help you move, use music that you like. If possible, work with someone you like as you learn.
Kinesthetic Left-Brain	Join in with others who are performing the sport or dance and follow along in a step-by-step way. Have a coach guide you through it, giving you step-by-step verbal directions and carry them out as you listen. Your kinesthetic sense will get an automatic feel for the movements and they will come easily and naturally for you. You can pick them up just by working with others who are performing in a step-by-step way.
Kinesthetic Right-Brain	You will learn the sport or dance by just jumping in and doing it with others. Observe the entire process first so you have the big picture or overview. Then get involved just by doing it. Learning a sport or dance by doing it comes easily for you, because by participating, you learn through trial and error. A coach can guide you where you need refinement. The action and movement of sports and dance and the fun of competition make this an easy way for you to learn.

Vocational Fields and Hobbies

There are numerous vocational fields and hobbies in which people are engaged for work and play, and these involve learning a skill that needs to be performed. This area encompasses construction, architecture, design, landscaping, interior decoration, plumbing, electrical engineering, painting, wallpapering, gardening, agriculture, farming, carpentry, building airplanes, trucks, or cars, delivering, driving, trucking, shipping, sales, marketing, crafts, textiles, sewing, knitting, fashion design, jewelry-making, modeling, art, music, machine repairs, the restaurant and food industry, entertainment, and numerous other fields. Learning any of these can become easy and quicker if the instruction is adapted to our own superlink. The following are adaptations to help accelerate learning of these fields through your superlink.

Visual Left-Brain	Read written instructions on how to perform the task. Enact each step as you read. The instructions should describe every small detail of movement required to perform the task successfully.
Visual Right-Brain	Look at illustrations, pictures, diagrams, photographs, or watch live demonstrations of the task. First see the entire process before going into each step. Find illustrations that pictorially show each movement. Photographs are better than videos unless you stop the action to get a clear view of each step.
Auditory Left-Brain	You need to hear each step of the directions aurally, then talk through the steps as you do them. Make sure they are broken down into every single movement you are required to do. Try to work with others so you can discuss the steps of the task. Tape-record or use a Dictaphone to record the instructions and again, until you remember them.

Auditory Right-Brain	Observe someone performing the entire task, getting a global overview of the process. Have them describe a few key movements using a few sensory words. Tape-record these instructions so you can play them back. Jump in and do the task, getting it by trial and error. Work with music you like. Talk through the key points of the steps with someone. Have someone observe you and tell you in a few simple sensory words how to adjust your performance of the task.
Tactile Left-Brain	In a step-by-step way, write down the instructions that you read, hear, or observe for the task you will have to do. Make sure you write each detailed step. Then enact each step, following your written notes. Get your feelings involved in the job, and as you learn, try to work with someone you like.
Tactile Right-Brain	Watch someone do the entire process of the task first. Then make sketches or drawings of the job. Follow your drawings as you perform the task. Try to involve your feelings in the process, and use music that you like to help you move. If possible, work with someone you like as you learn the job.
Kinesthetic Left-Brain	Join in with others who are performing the task and follow along in a step-by-step way. Have a coach guide you through it, giving you step-by-step verbal directions, and carry them out as you listen. Your kinesthetic sense will get an automatic feel for the job and it will come easily and naturally for you. You can pick it up just by working with others who are performing it in a step-by-step way.

| **Kinesthetic Right-Brain** | You will learn the task by just jumping in and doing it with others. Observe the entire process first so you have the big picture, or overview. Then just get involved by doing it. Learning by doing comes easily for you because you learn by trial and error. The action and movement of a skill or task makes this an easy way for you to learn. A coach can guide you where you need refinement. |

Recommended Reading

The Brain, Learning Styles, and Teaching

Brooks, Michael. *Instant Rapport.* New York: Warner Books, 1989.

Caine, Renate Nummela and Geoffrey Caine. *Making Connections: Teaching and the Human Brain.* Menlo Park, California: Addison-Wesley Publishing Company, Innovative Learning Publications, 1994.

Golden, Daniel. "Building a Better Brain." *National Geographic,* June 1994 (additional reporting: Anne Hollister and Sasha Nyary. Computer imagery by Alexander Tsiaras).

Halpern, Steven. *Comfort Zone.* Open Channel Sound Company (BMI), 1988.

_____ . *Music for Your PC.* Open Channel Sound Company (BMI), 1995.

_____ . *Sound Health.* New York: Harper and Row, 1985.

_____ . *Sound, Spirituality and Stress.* San Anselmo, Calif.: Steve Halpern's Inner Peace Music, 1996.

_____ . *Spectrum Suite.* Open Channel Sound Company (BMI), 1988.

_____ . *Tuning the Human Instrument: An Owner's Manual.* Spectrum Research Institute, 1978.

Hastenstab, Joseph K. and Connie Corcoran Wilson. *Training the Teacher as Champion.* Palo Alto, Calif.: Performance Learning Systems, 1988.

Hastenstab, Joseph K. *Performance Learning Systems: Teaching through Learning Channels.* Nevada City, Calif.: Performing Learning Systems, 1994.

_____ . *Cooperative Learning.* Nevada City, Calif.: Performance Learning Systems, 1993.

_____ . *Patterns for I.D.E.A.S.* Nevada City, Calif.: Performance Learning Systems, 1987.

_____ . *Keys to Motivation*. Nevada City, Calif.: Performance Learning Systems, 1990.

_____ . *Project T.E.A.C.H.* Nevada City, Calif.: Performance Learning Systems, 1989.

_____ . *Teaching the Skills for the 21st Century*. Nevada City, Calif.: Performance Learning Systems, 1994.

Linksman, Ricki. *Linksman Learning Style Preference Assessment and Brain Hemispheric Preference Assessment*. Naper-ville, Ill.: National Reading Diagnostics Institute, 1993.

Performance Learning Systems. *Learning Style Inventory*. Palo Alto, Calif.: Performance Learning Systems, 1995.

Russell, Peter. *The Brain Book*. New York: Plume, 1979.

Swerdlow, Joel L. "Quiet Miracles of the Brain," *National Geographic*, Vol. 187, No. 6, June 1995.

Sylwester, Robert. *A Celebration of Neurons: An Educator's Guide to the Human Brain*. Alexandria, Va.: Association for Supervision and Curriculum Development, 1995.

Thompson, Richard F. *The Brain: A Neuroscience Primer*. (2nd Edition). New York: W. H. Freeman and Company, 1993.

Vitale, Barbara Meister. *Free Flight: Celebrating Your Right Brain*. Torrance, Calif.: Jalmar Press, 1986.

_____ . *Unicorns Are Real: A Right-Brained Approach to Learning*. Calif.: Jalmar Press, 1982.

Reading and Comprehension Improvement

Linksman, Ricki. *Letter-Sound Relationship Test*. Naperville, Ill.: National Reading Diagnostics Institute, 1993.

_____ . *Passage Reading Test*. Naperville, Ill.: National Reading Diagnostics Institute, 1993.

_____ . *Solving Your Child's Reading Problems*. New York: Citadel Press, 1995.

_____ . *The Vowel and Consonant Dictionary*. Naperville, Ill.: National Reading Diagnostics Institute, 1993.

_____ . *The Vowel and Consonant Guide*. Naperville, Ill.: National Reading Diagnostics Institute, 1993.

Study Skills and Mind-Mapping

Buzan, Tony. *Use Both Sides of Your Brain*. New York: Dutton, 1983.

Multiple Intelligences

Armstrong, Thomas. *Seven Kinds of Smart: Identifying and Developing Your Many Intelligences*. New York: Plume, 1993.

Gardner, Howard. *Frames of Mind: The Theory of Multiple Intelligences*. New York: Basic Books, HarperCollins, 1983.

———. *The Unschooled Mind: How Children Think and How Schools Should Teach*. New York: Basic Books, HarperCollins, 1991.

Lazear, David. *Seven Ways of Knowing: Teaching for Multiple Intelligences*. (2nd ed.), Palatine, Ill.: IRI/Skylight Publications, 1991.

———. *Seven Ways of Teaching: The Artistry of Teaching with Multiple Intelligences*. Palatine, Ill.: IRI/Skylight Publications, 1991.

Typology (Psychological Types)

Hall, James A. *The Jungian Experience: Analysis and Individuation*. Toronto: Inner City Books, 1986.

Jung, C. G. "Psychological Types." In *Collected Works*, Vol. 6. Princeton: Princeton University Press, 1971.

Keirsey, David, and Marilyn Bates. *Please Understand Me: Character and Temperament of Types*. Del Mar, Calif.: Prometheus Nemesis Book Company, 1984.

Lawrence, Gordon D. *People Types and Tiger Stripes*. Gainesville, Fla.: Center for Applications of Psychological Type Inc., 1993.

Myers, Isabel B. *Myers-Briggs Type Indicator*. Palo Alto, Calif.: Consulting Psychological Press, 1962.

Myers, Isabel Briggs, with Peter B. Myers. *Gifts Differing: Understanding Personality Type*. Palo Alto, Calif.: Consulting Psychological Press, 1993.

Quenk, Naomi L. *Besides Ourselves: Our Hidden Personality in Everyday Life*. Palo Alto, Calif.: Consulting Psychological Press, 1993.

Stein, Murray, ed. *Jungian Analysis*. La Salle, Ill.: Open Court, 1994.

Index